THE XIAOMI WAY

THE XIAOMI WAY

THE XIAOMI WAY

Customer Engagement Strategies that Built One of the Largest Smartphone Companies in the World

Li Wanqiang

New York   Chicago   San Francisco   Lisbon   Athens   London
Madrid   Mexico City   Milan   New Delhi   San Juan
Seoul   Singapore   Sydney   Toronto

1 2 3 4 5 6 7 8 9 0   DOC   21 20 19 18 17 16

ISBN   978-1-25-958453-4
MHID   1-25-958453-4

e-ISBN   978-1-25-958454-1
e-MHID   1-25-958454-2

McGraw-Hill Education books are available at special quantity discounts to use as premiums and sales promotions or for use in corporate training programs. To contact a representative, please visit the Contact Us pages at www.mhprofessional.com.

Translated by Martha Avery, who divides her time between a tree farm in the Midwest and a cabin in the Rockies.

CONTENTS

HOW PIGS FLY: HELD UP BY A SENSE OF ENGAGEMENT!

One evening in early July, Li Wanqiang (Alee is his English name) came in to see me with a manuscript in his arms and said he was ready to hand over his assignment. He said, "Ten years ago, you asked me to write a book about the user experience and interface design. Well, it took me ten years, but I did it."

In 2000, Alee had just graduated from college and come to work at Kingsoft. We quickly recognized his talents as a software interface designer, and we asked him to organize an interface design team at the company. This was the first team working specifically on user-interface R&D in the entire industry. The team produced the interface design for such Kingsoft products as Antivirus and WPS (Writer, Presentation, and Spreadsheets, a suite of office-related software), which were well received in the market.

In 2004, I asked him to write a book and share his knowledge about user interface for the industry at large, so as to push it forward. He began the work and had finished around one-half when he was transferred to the Internet business department of Kingsoft. His job there was to launch the upgrade to a new Internet model, so he became quite busy and had to put the manuscript aside.

At the end of 2009, when he had quit his job in Kingsoft, he came to see me and said he was planning to become a commercial photographer. I in turn told him that I was planning to start a new company, and I wondered if he might be interested in joining me. He didn't pretend to think it over—he immediately agreed. Astonished, I asked him if he knew what I was going to make. Without hesitation, he said, "You are going to make smartphones."

Alee knew I was crazy about smartphones and that I had my own ideas about what to do with them.

It is true that I love playing with smartphones. More importantly, though, I have created software products for more than 20 years, and I have a lot of ideas about how to combine the two. Whenever I meet up with someone in a smartphone company, I bounce my ideas off him or her. Even 10 years ago, I was bouncing ideas off the vice president of global R&D for Nokia, when that company was at its height. What I have really wanted to do is create a company that gives the fans or enthusiasts a sense of engagement with the company as well. It seems to me that any company with real value in the future has to be this kind of company, in which users themselves engage in creating products.

Four years ago, when we were founding Xiaomi, the concept was to make the company feel like a small restaurant, a place where users could come inside and be a part of the scene. I felt this should be the case no matter how large the company might become in the future. Meanwhile, the boss should be a friend of every single customer who comes in to eat. This friendship model is the only business model that can be sustained over the long term.

We kept to that concept as we made our first product MIUI based on the Android system. Strictly speaking, MIUI was a smartphone operating system that was custom made to a deep degree on top of the Android system. The operating system was extremely complex. Very few people could bring it to a stage where you could begin to ask users their opinion about the results because the R&D cycle was so lengthy.

We realized that we needed to adopt the development model used by Internet software developers, and do it in phases. We could try putting out a new generation every week. The main problem with building the operating system was to understand users' needs, to understand what they really wanted, and then turn those things into an actual product. This also involved the issue of maintaining quality control; plus, there was the issue of putting something out every week.

Xiaomi put a lot of time and effort into thinking about how to do this. The company then became the first in the world to create the business model of making a new-generation operating system every week. To test this model, we gathered a group of users and asked them to play with and confirm the usefulness of the model. To figure out whether or not the business model was a good one, we kept the whole thing secret in the early period. We did zero publicity and made no sales. Our sole purpose was to conduct the experiment and see just how much "energy" we could generate from a model that was being sold based purely on word-of-mouth reputation.

Some people undoubtedly misunderstand Xiaomi. They think the company is what it is today because of a tremendous sales system for its smartphone. In fact, the very first press conference for Xiaomi was on August 16, 2011, which was one year after the launch of MIUI. By that time, MIUI already had 500,000 users. During that one-year period, Xiaomi did not undertake any sales activity at all—people may not be fully aware of that fact.

If pigs stand at the right place in the typhoon, they can indeed fly. All things depend on being aligned with the right forces. If you think of the founders of a start-up company as lucky pigs, the industry trends are the typhoon, and the engagement is the typhoon too.

The first year in Xiaomi, two things were tested and thoroughly demonstrated. First, we learned that users engaged in product development could indeed lead to our making good products. Second, good products could be sold through the word-of-mouth reputation of users. This corroboration then taught Xiaomi two important lessons: first, the company needed to interact with users to produce good products, and second, it needed to rely on word-of-mouth reputation to carry out the marketing and sales. At the core of the Xiaomi philosophy is developing the users' sense of engagement in the process. It is through their sense of engagement that we can complete the R&D process, accomplish marketing and promotion of the products, accomplish user servicing, and in the process make Xiaomi into a very "cool" brand, which brings young people together. In the process of developing the company, this has been the most important concept. In a nutshell, it is to "think of users as friends."

Alee was one of the cofounders of Xiaomi. In the early period, he was responsible for R&D on the MIUI, and then later he became responsible for the Xiaomi network called mi.com. I deeply appreciate the way he has found time in his busy schedule to write this book, *The Xiaomi Way*. It pulls together the experiences and shares them with everyone. I feel that certain things in the structuring of the development of user engagement are particularly significant for the industry as a whole. We call it the "three-on-three principles of engagement," which include three layers of strategy and three layers of tactics, as discussed in the book.

I am also very moved by the fact that Alee remembered his promise over all these years and, what's more, that he kept that promise.

Lei Jun, CEO of Xiaomi

CHAPTER 1

A SENSE OF ENGAGEMENT

The Internet and the Word-of-Mouth Reputation

How do you lock in the first million users? To do so requires different strategies in today's Internet businesses.

FIGURE 1.1 *On the Internet, word-of-mouth reputation is king.*

Kingsoft was founded in 1988. In the age of traditional software, it was the leading brand in China. I entered the company in 2000 as a designer, and Lei Jun, who was CEO, led us to create many ferocious strategies.

At the time, we focused a lot on very important project management. For example, WPS, the large office-suite software, and a large-scale online game that Kingsoft put out called for an enormous amount of low-level software development. Each new version took years to complete, and each would have landmark nodes along the way, such as M0, M1, M2, and so on. It took at least half a year to get beyond each node.

Even at that time, however, Kingsoft was very conscious of the importance of the user experience, and in 2000 the company set up the first "human-machine interface design team" in China. Our method of interacting with users was via focus groups. Every quarter, or every half year, we would assemble a few dozen users and conduct in-person discussions on different products. Another method was to have the customer service team collect user opinions. The team would write these up into reports and pass them on to product managers every week. The product managers would put them into their reports for "project teams," who passed them on to the vice president in charge who passed them on to senior management. The cycle for this entire process of reviewing user opinions generally took more than a month.

Products not only went through much research in pre-production but also received massive marketing when on the market. During the Kingsoft period, we very consciously used all three military tactics—"air, naval, and ground forces"—to attack the market. We called it a *storm attack*.

The so-called air, naval, and ground forces operated as follows: the "air force" aimed at the entirety of the market, the "ground forces" did offline promotion through PR teams, while the "naval forces" worked in cooperation with selected sales channels.

At that time, we generally would attach a highpoint title to the project, like Red Storm Authorized Version, Dragon-Marching Century, Lofty Sentiments on Autumn Evenings, and so on. We first would get the concept fully established before launching it on the market.

We then would raise the decibel level of our promotion as we turned it into a full-scale promotion event. These marketing activities were extremely successful and quite gratifying. For example, in 1999, Red Storm Authorized Version produced by Kingsoft sold 1.1 million copies in the first three months after being released, which was an unprecedented record at that time for a non-pirated version of software in China.

In concert with this marketing strategy, Kingsoft set up internal management systems to "mobilize staff for specific battles." During particularly large campaigns, we would meet every morning for pep talks. All parts of the company, different departments as well as different business lines, would come together to "attack the stronghold" in terms of both product development and sales and marketing. Kingsoft had a classic kind of militaristic culture. If the battle was going well, people would "lift a glass and celebrate." If it was going badly, people would "defy death to help one another." Teams had a well-disciplined ability to perform, and a tremendous sense of brotherhood.

Whenever the business had problems, this sense of brotherhood was like a powerful weapon. At the time, we had an engineer named Hai Zhou, who now serves as head of engineering at mi.com. Back then, we were working together on the product called PowerWord, a kind of bilingual dictionary. He talked to me about leaving the company twice within the space of one year because many companies were trying to poach him to come over to work for them. The way I handled this was as follows. Each time he mentioned leaving us, I would ask him out to dinner at 5 p.m. We would then eat and drink until we all got drunk, until 5 a.m. the next morning. The morning of the second late night he was so full of remorse about the very thought of leaving that he never brought the subject up again.

The business methods used by Kingsoft at the time played an extremely important role as precursors for the whole industry in China. In terms of product development, marketing, and team management, they became the reigning model for that period in China's software industry.

Kingsoft went public in Hong Kong in 2007. Since this marked success in the milepost model of accomplishment, Lei Jun, having rendered meritorious service, left Kingsoft to become an angel investor. He then founded Xiaomi in 2010. Several years after being listed, Kingsoft's Internet business slowed down, and Lei Jun returned to serve as CEO in 2011. Kingsoft's capitalization on the market then gradually went to a new high of USD 3 billion. The number of people using the mobile version of WPS Office broke through the 100 million mark, and it became the main office software suite. In May 2014, a subsidiary called Cheetah Mobile under the banner of Kingsoft was carved out and listed on the market independently. In the mobile Internet age, the Kingsoft brand had now become active once again but at a whole new level.

Lei Jun has described what he believes are the three critical steps in developing a successful start-up: select a large market, form an outstanding team of people, and make sure you have access to an unlimited amount of money. The question then becomes, "What has been the difference between Kingsoft and Xiaomi?"

When Kingsoft and Xiaomi were being founded, both chose well in terms of business orientation, and both formed the most outstanding teams possible. The differences between the two are as follows:

1. **Xiaomi was able to obtain plenty of money in its early start-up period.** During the Kingsoft period, the company's WPS product was everywhere, and the penetration rate of its set-top box software exceeded 80 percent. Given the widespread practice of pirating in the country, however, Kingsoft did not make much money. It also had not been able to attract a sufficient amount of investment from the capital markets. As a result, Kingsoft had to fight each battle just in order to fund the next battle. Money that it earned from WPS went into the product Siba, and money from Siba went into the product antivirus and games. In the end, the games earned money, which was what enabled Kingsoft to list successfully on the market. In this process of fighting each battle just to fund the next step, however, it was hard to sustain deeper and more penetrating business models. As the Internet standards shifted, going from one generation to the next, the company

was forced to think mainly about how to fund its existing business. It could not make long-term decisions about generational shift.

2. **In founding Xiaomi, Lei Jun asked us to focus on just one thing: word-of-mouth reputation.** This change in the way of thinking about products and markets was like asking everyone to erase the operating system in his or her brain and start over. We put out a new generation every week instead of every year. Now, we all were asked to be involved in customer service instead of being involved in all-out battle. R&D on the user experience was no longer a matter of monthly or quarterly meetings but rather a matter of daily communications with users. The "storm attack" mode of sales and promotion was now transformed into "penetrating interaction." Each function added to the phone was to permeate the users' daily activities soundlessly. Marketing strategy no longer pursued a highpoint, and instead, we spoke plainly and directly.

In 2008, Lei Jun brought forth what we called the *four-word formula* for the Internet. In Chinese, this used seven words to describe four concepts: focus, ultimate excellence, word-of-mouth reputation, and speed. The first two of these were product goals. The last, word-of-mouth reputation, was the absolute core idea behind the whole Internet. Speed was the principle applied to action. The traditional approach had always been to do things slowly so as to do them right, as encapsulated in the phrase "Slow work yields fine products." In contrast, the "extremist style" of the Internet was generated in the midst of fast-speed generational shift. Internet technology changes by the day, and this forces an extremely fast pace of "rebooting" the entire industry. In just 20 years, China has been through three stages of technological change: portals, Web 2.0, and mobile Internet.

The age of mobile Internet forces us to be fast. Companies that are not fast will be washed out of the market. This term *fast*, however, also refers to a method. It is not a goal in itself, but rather it is the necessary result of the logic of a new industry that incorporates the psychology of consumers. In the past, after handing a product over to

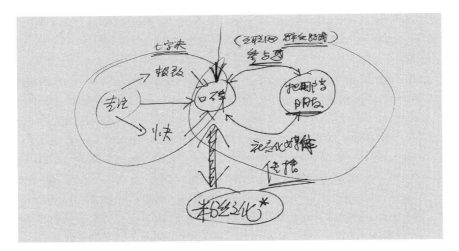

FIGURE 1.2 *Lei Jun's Scribbled Notes on Internet Thinking*

users, a company generally felt that its contact with those users was finished. Now, handing over the product is seen as just the beginning. In what follows, the company has to have constant interaction with users and enable them to engage in the ongoing process of improving the product.

The reason "word-of-mouth reputation" is king on the Internet is that today's users select products mostly by the word-of-mouth reputation of those products.

Google has incorporated this wisdom into their operations. When Google released Gmail in 2004, it relied exclusively on word-of-mouth promotion. It issued just a few thousand beta-test user accounts. If anyone else wanted to use the system, they had to be invited by one of these people. The number of "invitee codes" was limited, and the codes soon became highly sought after around the globe. People were trading all kinds of things to get them. The asking price for a Gmail account even got to 75 pounds sterling on eBay. I myself went to a lot of trouble at the time to get a Gmail invitee code. This was the first time I really understood the way that word-of-mouth reputation was being used by Google.

Quite a few products that have emerged on the Taobao site (part of the Alibaba Group) have also relied on word-of-mouth promotion.

For example, the Handu Group brand relies on being fast in following up on fashion design, and it has become the key site female users recommend in many of the online buying communities. Another product, Yunifang, sells mainly by claiming to be made of only natural products and minerals, and so it has become the number one skincare product on Taobao. A third example is the brand Three Squirrels nut products on Taobao. I and many of my friends have personally witnessed the phenomenon that the more something starts selling, the hotter it gets if one is using word-of-mouth promotion.

Of course we have always used the recommendations of friends or authorities to make decisions about what to buy. Such recommendations were not, however, what drove mainstream buying. Today, behind this idea that word-of-mouth is king is the fact that information transmission as we now know it has gone through several major changes:

1. Information has gone from being asymmetrical to being symmetrical.
2. The speed of information transmission has increased dramatically, and it has reached unprecedented dimensions in terms of its scope of influence.
3. Internet information spreads in decentralized ways through social media, and each common person is an information node so that each has the possibility of being an opinion leader.

The traditional setting for word-of-mouth promotion was, for example, a hair salon in which people chatted as they had their hair done. The speed at which their information traveled was slow, and it was also easily interrupted and sometimes actually stopped. On social media platforms such as Weibo and WeChat, not only are information links among people flattened and equalized but the speed at which their information travels has gone up thousands of times. Instead of being reckoned in terms of months or days, as before, it is now reckoned in terms of minutes and seconds. In the past, the release of a piece of news first had to come from a centralized news source and be broadly reported before it had any social effect. Nowadays, a piece of news is often a hot topic among the public before it gets picked up by the media.

Traditionally, it was logical for companies to try to sell via advertising and public relations because information dissemination was asymmetrical. You had to try to make your voice heard. Social media has now flattened everything, however, while the speed of information transmission has exploded. The "radius" of information dissemination has increased by hundreds and thousands of times, which means that events or situations can frequently become famous overnight.

The way in which information transmission has become symmetrical increases the ability of users to "vote with their feet." A company may brag as much as it likes about how good its products or services are, but what the public says is what counts. Good and bad news can be shared alike by a public that is connected through all kinds of community networks. Meanwhile, the impartial and egalitarian nature of information has also given the public space of the Internet the immense power of "self-cleansing" by public opinion. It is much harder to make false information appear to be true, and it is hard to make true information look false.

Changes in information transmission also mean that the habits by which users get information are changing. The ubiquitous presence of mobile devices and the convenience of the Internet mean that every person has become a source of information on what to eat, how to dress, where to go, and what to do. People have become quite accustomed to letting their friends know about their immediate experience in consuming whatever it is they are consuming. For example, when you go to a restaurant with friends these days, instead of picking up your chopsticks when the first dish arrives, you take photos. You share the photos on WeChat. Within minutes, your friends in your Internet community will have "liked," "teased," or reposted.

In the new age of mobile Internet, therefore, we have to make use of word-of-mouth reputation, and that means we simply have to be good at using social media.

The Iron Triangle of the Word-of-Mouth Reputation

The secret of success in Internet thinking is "focus." Only if you remain focused on something can you be fast. Only if you are fast can you achieve "ultimate excellence." Only if you have achieved ultimate excellence can you get a good word-of-mouth reputation. Only those who live by word-of-mouth reputation on the Internet survive. People say that Xiaomi is good at selling, but in fact it is good at word-of-mouth approbation. Essentially, Xiaomi's marketing is word-of-mouth marketing.

As I understand the term, word-of-mouth reputation is similar to the three essential parts of power-driven systems. I call these parts of the *iron triangle* the *engine, accelerator,* and *transmission*:

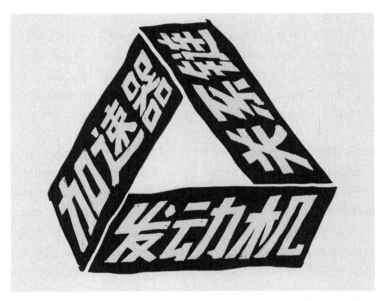

FIGURE 1.3 *The Iron Triangle of Word-of-Mouth Reputation*

1. Engine: products
2. Accelerator: social media
3. Transmission: customer relations

If a company wants to have a good reputation, its *engine* has to be good products. They are the foundation of all foundations. The quality of products is "1." Without it, any attempt to sell a brand comes to "0."

Having a good reputation means you need to enable more people to know about your products more quickly, which means you have to master the art of social media. Social media represents the *accelerator* of word-of-mouth reputation.

When I was in charge of the team creating the first MIUI project for Xiaomi, Lei Jun asked me, "Can you get to 1 million customers without spending a single cent?" The only way to do that was to grab hold of word-of-mouth reputation. Without any money to spend, what you have to do is get people to extol your products on their own initiative. Have them voluntarily recommend your products to all those around them. Then all you have to do is make sure your products and service are excellent.

In August 2010, we had only a hundred users when the first version of MIUI was released. These were the core users at the heart of the word-of-mouth process. By August 2011, when the actual Mi was released, MIUI already possessed 500,000 fans. In terms of learning about word-of-mouth transmittal of information, Xiaomi had already accumulated sufficient initial momentum to move forward.

When MIUI was first established, three nodes, or links, in the process were of ultimate importance. These three represented the storyline and subject behind its word-of-mouth reputation. These nodes endowed products with qualities that gave people something to talk about.

"Speed" was the first item in word-of-mouth approval. Usage had to be smooth, easy, and fast. We began by embedding the Android operating system deeply into products. At the time, MIUI was mainly read-only memory (ROM) for installing firmware on a mobile device. Superficially, the user was using the smartphone hardware, but in fact the great majority of the operational experience was essentially coming from the software. At the time, most firmware for mobile devices was made by individual people or small teams. They did not have enough stamina or power on their own to make real improvements to the lowest levels. As soon as we appeared, however, we focused on speed by improving the speed of frames on the screen. We made sure the screen had a sense of smooth movement so that it went from 30 frames per second to 40 to 60. We gradually dealt with every complaint put forward by users. We improved the phoning and texting touch pad so that it gave a better experience and was faster. For example, when issuing a text to a frequent recipient, instead of the standard three to five steps, we made it possible to send the text in two steps.

"Good looking" was the second item in word-of-mouth approval. At the time, and compared to Apple, the Android system was decidedly ugly due to its primitive interface. We first improved the programming to speed up the system, which also made it better looking, in around three or four months. One year later, the theme of the MIUI was ready for the stage of compiling. If you had enough capacity, meaning numbers of people, you could make the theme do whatever you wanted. It could be said that in the MIUI design theme, either openness or deepness, we were quite successful throughout all of the Android system.

"Openness" was the third item in word-of-mouth approval. We allowed users to download the Android system and edit their own custom-made versions. How was this helpful? Openness allowed users from many different countries to "come in," to the extent that they issued their own versions of MIUI in English, Spanish, Portuguese, and so on. This openness tactic drew in many fans who then disseminated MIUI on a deeper level. Meanwhile, the acceptance of overseas users influenced the spread of the system in the domestic market, similar to the way exporting affects domestic consumption as well.

After winning approval on the above three points, we chose a highly effective channel for disseminating the product. That is, we used social media as the accelerator for spreading word on the product. The first 500,000 users of MIUI were generated through the bulletin board system (BBS), but the next 500,000 were achieved through such social media as blogs.

The question then becomes, "What is the ideal relationship between the company and users?" Since thousands of users all have their own ideas about things, why should they choose your product? After approving of your product themselves, why should they voluntarily go on to recommend it to others and help you sell it?

Community networks are based on a trust relationship between individuals, and the movement or passage of information from one to another represents the transmission of that trust. The higher the degree of trust that a user feels toward a company, the more broadly that person will spread the word.

In traditional business, what you would often see was a relationship that asked the company to yield to the customer. The customer was God or perhaps one's parents, as long as the customer was willing to pull out his or her money and buy your product. Or you would see a relationship that asked the user to yield to the company, as if to say, "Our products are the best, and if you don't like it, you can just go away."

As I see it, both of the above attitudes weaken the relationship with users. Both make it hard for the user to generate any kind of instinctive liking and enthusiasm for your product. The traditional mode of doing things turns the relationship between a user and the product into a naked matter of money. Once the transaction is done, the relationship between company and user is cut off—some companies even hope to have nothing further to do with the customer once he or she has bought the product. After all, further entanglements might involve all kinds of post-purchase demands, disputes, costs, and PR crises.

Instead, a company has to make friends with its users. Only friends will really help you pass on the word and support you with their word-of-mouth approval. "Making friends" creates a highly trusting relationship with users.

The guiding thought in Xiaomi regard to user relationships is, "Make friends with your users."

You want to have your employees become users of the product as well, so that they turn their friends into users but also so that they are all involved in customer service and encouraged to make friends with all other users.

The mode of operations in Xiaomi encourages users to "enter into the process," given its openness with regard to the operating platform as well as service. Making friends with users is equivalent to playing with them. It is the opposite of issuing products from on high and then conducting formula-driven surveys to find out what

给用户下跪   让用户下跪

和用户做朋友

FIGURE 1.4 *Three Relationships with Users: (1) "The users are gods."*
(2) "Let users yield to the company." (3) "Make friends with the users."

people think. Playing with users as though they were friends, talking
about products through blogs, on MiTalk (a kind of communication
software that was developed by Xiaomi) or Weibo, and connecting
with people are all ways of generating demand and disseminating
the product.

The transformation in business models, to making friends with
customers, is made necessary by the fact that we are living in an age

when you cannot simply "sell" a product. Rather, what you are selling is a sense of engagement in the product.

The Three-on-Three Principles of Engagement

In private, a lot of my friends ask me, "How does Xiaomi get users to 'detonate' such an incredibly explosive spread of information on social media?"

My answer is: engagement, engagement, and engagement.

FIGURE 1.5 *The Three-on-Three Principles of Engagement*

The core concept behind conducting business successfully over the Internet is that word-of-mouth reputation is king. Since what users are thinking is of the essence, you want to have users feel that they are part of the whole process.

It's like the attack from a different dimension in the science-fiction novel *The Three-Body Problem*. You are dealing with a parallel universe—in simple terms, all you can say is that the world has changed.

Consumer psychology has gone through a massive transformation in the past few decades in terms of how people decide on what to buy. At the beginning, people used a *functional model*, then later a *brand model*, and in more recent years the popular thing has been an *experience model*. In contrast to all of these, the discovery of Xiaomi, and the process in which it is itself immersed, is what we call *participatory consumption*.

When material goods were scarce, people bought things to satisfy certain functions. Back then, it didn't matter which brand it was. The key thing was that a timepiece told time. As society developed and things became more abundant, advertising companies emerged and differentiated among them by emphasizing brands. Brands became the key factor in the world of goods. For a while, brand consulting companies, advertising companies, design companies, and so on were riding the wave.

Motorola invented the smartphone, but Nokia popularized it. In around the year 2000, Nokia used the idea of "making technology human centered" to globalize its brand. This branding was so successful at penetrating people's consciousness that Nokia soon surpassed Motorola and Edison with unprecedented market share in consumer electronics.

Branding operations went through an almost insane era, with health products and "white spirit" being the most outstanding examples. As many will remember, ads for some health products reached down to every town and village in China. Companies even pasted ads on pigpens. Some brands had their glory days for a while, but when the experience model of consumption came along, many of these brands disappeared without a trace.

As the super-mall type of selling venue began to replace the old department store, the age of "experiencing consumption" had arrived. People were invited to "try a little" as a way to get them to buy—try a little of this food, put this on and see how it looks. "Does this smartphone suit you? Come on in to the shop, and see all the things it can do."

In order to enable the user to have a deeper sense of engagement, from the outset Xiaomi asked users to engage in the development of products as well as in the marketing operations. We gradually discovered that the age of participatory consumption had in fact already arrived. What's more, it satisfied this whole new consumer psychology of people.

FIGURE 1.6 *The Evolution of the Concept of Consumption: Functional → Brand → Experiencing → Participatory*

Enabling users to participate satisfied the psychological need of young people to "get into the scene" and to voice their desire to "influence the world." Prior to this, the phenomenon was seen in such things as user-generated content (UGC), through which the users generated the content, with the famous B Station (Bilibili.tv) being the classic example of a cartoons-and-comics cultural circle. Young people use a variety of methods to re-create their own versions or sequels, and they have thereby created a whole new low-brow-culture language system that is unique.

How do you generate this sense of engagement quickly, in terms of a company's operations?

Building a sense of engagement involves opening up the processes of making products, providing services, creating brands, and generating sales. It involves inviting the users in to all these processes and setting up a brand that is "touchable" and "possess-able," and that allows the users themselves to grow together with the brand. I sum this concept up in three strategies and three tactics. Inside the company, we call these the *three-on-three principles of engagement*:

	Open participation modes	Modes of interactive design	Events for spreading word-of-mouth reputation	Participating customers	Frequency of activities	Number of people participating	Page number
Orange Friday	• Demand for MIUI products • Testing of MIUI products • Launching MIUI products	• Discussion on forums • Five changes every week • Honorary developers team • Developers' Edition and Stable Edition	• Sharing of successful upgrades • Reports on experiences • Weekly functions and announcements • Mini-videos about the "Benefactors of 100 dreams"	Customers who use the MIUI Developers Edition	Weekly	One million	P25
Red Tuesday	Purchasing on the Xiaomi Network	Advance orders, Snatch purchases	• Making public the results of each open-purchasing event • Sharing in prearranged meetings	Customers who purchase cellphones	Weekly	One million	P41
Popcorn	• Selection of locations for offline activities • Design of on-site activities	• Voting via forums • Plan for activities on forums • Meetings within cities in various parts of China	• Sharing of on-site Wechat messages • Annual popcorn event, Popcorn Magazine	Customers who are active on Xiaomi forums	Monthly	10,000	P76
Red-mi cellphone	Initial online release	• Guessing what products will be released • Re-transmitting and prearranged meetings	Transmitting advance orders of the 7.5 million Red-mi team	Customers on QQ Space	One-off events	Ten million	P143
Ad for "Our Age"	Initial online response	• Selecting superior gift items • Making individualized recommendations	• Sharing of individualized comments on Wechat • Transmittal of stories about making advertisements	Customers on the Internet	One-off events	One million	P105
Xiaomi system	Collecting ideas for improving service	Transmitting and rechecking internal system	Public notices and awards for all employees	Employees in the Xiaomi service system	Daily	One thousand	P175
Open day at Xiaomi	• Factory production • Shipping out of product • On-site servicing at Xiaomi Home	• Going on-site to look things over • Release of product	Transmitting of self-generated media	Highly qualified customers and people in the media	Once a season		P115

FIGURE 1.7 *The Three-on-Three Principles of Engagement*

Three strategies. Create products that are "in," turn users into fans, promote products through We Media.

Three tactics. Open R&D to users, create interactive designs, and promote through word-of-mouth.

"Create products that are 'in'" is a product strategy. At the planning stage of making products, you have to be bold enough to decide on just one. And if you're going to make that product, you want it to be number one in the market. Without having a product line that is consolidated, it is hard to gain any scale effect because resources are too dispersed to generate that sense of engagement.

"Turn users into fans" is a user strategy. Behind the ability to elicit a sense of engagement is the mantra "trust." This means moving a weak relationship with users in the direction of a stronger relationship. Building the Mi Fans culture means asking employees to be the fans of the product first and then enabling users to gain benefits from that. The initial incentive is shared functionality and information, shared interests, so we often say that being "teased" also demonstrates a kind of engagement. Benefits that follow include the kudos from fixing problems, among others. Sustainability comes from whatever enables both the company and the user to have a shared feeling of engagement.

"Promote through We Media" is a content strategy. The decentralization of the Internet has eliminated authority and also the asymmetry of information dissemination. Using We Media allows the company itself to become an information node on the Internet, and it allows for faster and flatter transmission of information—and because of that, it requires that the company internally restructure itself to become flatter as well. Each employee as well as each user is encouraged to become a spokesperson for the product. Creating content must abide by the idea that Internet-based operations should be useful, emotionally engaging, and interactive. "Only useful information" means "Avoid too much information." Each piece of information should have individualized emotional appeal in order to lead the user to interact with it, engage in it, and share it with a wider audience.

"Open R&D to users" means opening up the processes of making products, providing services, creating brands, and conducting sales. It involves sifting through and selecting links that allow both the company and the user to benefit. Only if both sides benefit is the participatory interaction sustainable. Open nodes should be based on the demand for functionality. The more that demand is inelastic, the more people will participate.

"Create an interactive design" means develop a design that corresponds to open nodes. Interactive recommendations should follow the design philosophy of being "simple, beneficial, interesting, and real." As in the process of making products, the whole process of interactive design must be an ongoing process of improvement. In the spring of 2014, an activity exploded on the scene called WeChat Lucky Money that is a perfect case of interactive design. By grabbing onto red packets, people could gain certain benefits. It was fun and also very simple.

"Promote through word-of-mouth" means that you first need to sift through and select the most supportive users of your product. Within a small circle of those people, you can get a sense of engagement "fermenting." Then you can turn content that has been created interactively into topics that can be transmitted out as an "incident." You enable the word-of-mouth to achieve a kind of fission that begins to influence more and more people. At the same time, you increase the sense of accomplishment of those who have been participating all along, and you allow them to enjoy the storm attack effect—that is, the feeling of being a part of the power of the vortex.

There are two main pathways of spreading the word. One is planting mechanisms in open products that encourage users to share in the process. Two mobile games created in 2013 did this extremely well. One was called Crazy Guessing Figure, and the other was called Find Something: Where Is My Goal? Every day there would be several tens of thousands of lines of information from the content that would be simplified and then shared via Weibo and WeChat, among other forms of social media. The other pathway is to use the process of interaction between users and official media to discover a topic that is then transmitted as an incident by pursuing it more deeply.

Why is it that different companies have radically different results from the same kind of tiger-catching approach? Also, why is it that some participatory events fizzle out after users try them a few times, so that the events are not sustainable? The main reason is that the approach is adopted superficially, without any in-depth thought for strategy. Strategy represents the decision either to do something and stick with it, or not to do something. Tactics are a matter of how to do it, on an operational level. In terms of users, strategies are the lower part of the iceberg that is not visible whereas tactics are the upper part of the iceberg that they can see. People have a greater visceral understanding and emotional feel for this part of the iceberg. In later chapters, I use specific cases to describe how we approach different kinds of users with respect to products and services and how we foster a sense of engagement in different scenarios.

In the four years since Xiaomi was founded, we have constantly expanded the depth and breadth of our understanding of engagement through actual practice. The results are already being applied not only to products and sales but also to the operations of the company as a whole. We have experimented with quite a few ways to ensure that a sense of engagement gets into the very bloodstream of every user and every employee.

Within Xiaomi itself, we have created a well-functioning system that allows us to improve products based on user responses. Xiaomi does not use key performance indicators (KPIs) or performance testing, so employee motivation is not driven by reaching performance goals. Furthermore, employee motivation does not rely on the boss alone. What drives performance is purely and simply these user responses.

C. K. Prahalad, the author of the book *The Future of Competition: Co-Creating Unique Value with Customers,* has noted that the company-centered type of innovation is already disappearing. Instead, consumers are playing a larger and larger role in the process of creating value by using the unique experience of each individual. Because of this, companies must establish new organizational structures.

A sense of engagement is of utmost importance, as I understand things. It indicates that consumer demand has undergone a once-and-for-all critical transition. For the first time, consumer demand has transcended the product itself. It is no longer limited by the attributes of the product, but rather, it has extended its rationale to social attributes: when you buy something today, you are not simply buying what the thing itself can do, but rather what you can do with the thing. Your purchase provides you with a possible new experience, something that you can feel a part of.

CHAPTER 2

PRODUCT

The User Model Is Greater Than Any Engineering Model

"Can you set up a development team that has 100,000 people in it?"

I had this crazy idea when I was working on MIUI. At the time, our development team had just over 20 people in it. MIUI was the first real product of Xiaomi, and it was also the first to experiment with this whole idea of user engagement (Figure 2.1).

用户模式大于一切工程模式

FIGURE 2.1 *The user model is greater than any engineering model.*

In order to enable users to come into the product development process in an in-depth way, we designed an Internet development model that we called Orange Friday (Figure 2.2). The gist of this idea was that the MIUI team would revise the system and put out a new version every week, through interaction with users on Internet bulletin board systems (BBSs).

FIGURE 2.2 *Orange Friday: An Internet Style of Software Development*

After making sure we were able to maintain the stability of basic functions, we allowed all ideas and functions to go out to users in a very open way, whether they were great ideas or not so great, and whether they were well-developed functions or not well developed. Every Friday afternoon, on schedule, we put a new version of MIUI on our website, accompanied by the orange-colored Xiaomi symbol.

The following Tuesday, MIUI would allow users who had tried out the new version to send in their *four-box experience reports*. From the very beginning, we were receiving upward of 10,000 responses, and by now we have hundreds of thousands of people participating in this process every week. Through reviewing these reports, we could assemble information on which functions users liked most and which they felt were not good enough, and we knew which had any hope at all of being disseminated to a broader public. Meanwhile, inside the company, we set up a prize called the MIPOP Prize. The team that had created the functions that had received the most positive votes in the previous week won the prize. This prize was not just a bucket of MIPOP—it was the sense of glory that came from being called a "god" by everyone.

The zero-distance connection between users and employees via BBS allowed users to approve of certain functions directly, which naturally pleased the teams who created those functions. When a given function was teased by users, or worse yet, when it was criticized, the product manager or the software engineer responsible for that function did not have to hold meetings to try to motivate his team. He would find them working overtime, putting everything they had into doing better the next time.

Our official team of over a hundred software engineers constituted the core of the 100,000-strong Internet development team that was set up through the use of BBS (Figure 2.3). Around the perimeter of this core was another tier of 1,000 highly professional reviewers and checkers, who were considered honorary insiders. The most active users were those who used the prototype, around 100,000 people who were dedicated to improving its functions. The outer perimeter was composed of the thousands upon thousands of users of the "stable version" of MIUI. Each of those tiers actively participated in improving the upgrading of MIUI in its own way. Among all these people, our honorary insiders were called The Honorables.

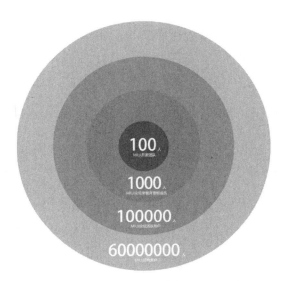

FIGURE 2.3 *The Internet Model for a Software Development Team*

Because of the various tiers, or levels, the constantly upgrading structure of MIUI was formed of different versions. There was a *gray-level version* and various stair-stepped versions. The fastest innovations came from the honorary insiders, and these were incorporated into the *inside test version*. That version would get upgraded daily. It had the fastest rate of testing new functions and eliminating bugs. The second fastest innovations came from the *development version*, which would get upgraded every week. After that came the *stable version*. This would generally get upgraded every one to two months.

Users would eagerly wait for the new version of MIUI to come out every Friday. These fans loved to install a new operating system, a new firmware, in their phone, to experience the new things and to test new functions. Maybe this Orange Friday's version would include something they themselves had designed! Or it might incorporate a bug they had worked out, one they had discovered. The prospect gave people who were deeply immersed in this process a great deal of satisfaction.

Many of the functional designs proposed for MIUI were put to users on a BBS to discuss or vote on. In four years of MIUI releases, the company gathered a total of more than 100 million user response posts. If you had printed them out on paper and connected them together, the length of the paper would have been close to the diameter of the earth.

Use the Three-on-Three Principles of Engagement

1. **Open R&D to users.** Except for portions of the program that were written in engineering code, all other product demand, testing, and releases were provided to users in an open way. This kind of openness was beneficial to both the company and users. We constantly improved the versions according to users' opinions, while users were able to get the functions and products they really wanted.
2. **Create an interactive design.** Based on the needs as expressed on the BBS, these changes were incorporated in a revised version put out every Orange Friday.

3. **Promote through word-of-mouth.** Promotional activities included internal mechanisms to encourage the sharing of MIUI, and they included events that we collected resources to fund. For the very first 100 users who participated in beta testing, we made a micro-movie called *Benefactors of 100 Dreams*, which was a "magnifier" that expanded the sense of engagement.

In building a process that had many more participants, we had to reduce the costs of user engagement as much as possible and also keep from "co-modifying" it or trying to make products out of it as the system was being developed. We regarded every weekly upgrade as an opportunity to consider how to reduce the memory costs. Having users transmit their user reports in the form of a four-box report was due to this consideration for costs.

It was precisely because of such mechanisms for in-depth engagement by users that MIUI was able to receive such astonishing rates of word-of-mouth approval and such incredible growth rates. The word-of-mouth approval gained by the MIUI experience was also later to be the foundation for the explosive numbers of people using Mi. On August 16, 2010, when the first version of MIUI was released, there were a mere 100 users. We had pulled in each of them from a third-party BBS. They had come based purely on word-of-mouth reputation, for we had not spent a cent on advertising. Nor had we done any "exchange of traffic" with other sites to get them to come. By August 16, 2011, when MIUI had been out for a full year, it already had 500,000 users.

Consumers are also producers. As Chris Anderson has said in his book *The Long Tail*, in the past, there was always a distinction between professionals and amateurs. In the future, however, it will be harder and harder to separate these two categories or to deal with them as separate things. With Xiaomi, at least, this separation is hard.

Wikipedia is the result of this kind of user model. The writers and editors of *Wikipedia* are not experts who were painstakingly chosen for these jobs, but rather, they are all kinds of enthusiasts, fanciers, and spectators. Yet these have people created a superlative product.

Under this kind of model, users not only use the products but they also "possess" the products. This *sense of possession* means that they not only eliminate problems when they find them but they also make every effort to engage in improving the product. "Everyone is a product manager."

The person in charge of engineering in Xiaomi is Huang Jiangji (who is also known as KK), and he is one of the alliance of founders of the company. KK originally worked at Microsoft. One day, he began to compare the differences in the beliefs held by Microsoft versus those held by Xiaomi and the two companies' development models.

He felt that Microsoft was unequaled in the early days in terms of human talent and internal processes. It took between 5,000 and 6,000 developers to put out each version of the Microsoft operating system. One can imagine 5,000 or 6,000 of the most acutely intelligent software developers, and they were divided into small groups, with each group composed of 5 people in a 311 structure—that is, for every 3 engineers, there was a product manager and an evaluator or tester. However, in this process, the voice of the user and the engagement of the user were essentially zero.

Microsoft garnered massive success in the PC era. In the Internet era, however, it began to face setbacks. At that time, KK was upset by this, and he wasn't sure why it was happening. Google, Facebook, and other newly founded companies, and even some smaller companies, were developing very quickly, even though they were faced with the competitive pressure of Microsoft. In some respects, these new companies were even surpassing Microsoft. KK wondered what the reasons might be.

KK kept wondering why Microsoft was not up to speed in certain new spheres of business in particular. Should the company consider a new development model? The reason he wondered about this is that Microsoft had always aimed for the kind of development model that was "perfect and complete." In this kind of model, one was not allowed to make mistakes. The time cycles were so tight and so strictly adhered to that if you wanted to implement the overall plan, nobody could make a mistake. This in itself was a problem.

After becoming one of the founders of Xiaomi, KK began to recognize the short stave in Microsoft's bucket, the thing that was preventing it from holding more water. He described Microsoft's development strategy as "3110." The first three digits could be multiplied by as many figures as you might like, but in the development process, the final digit, representing user input, remained zero.

What is the best product development model for the Internet age?

Xiaomi has come up with its own answer to that question: the user model. In industries that aim at consumers as their end point, the user model is more significant than any possible engineering model.

First Deal with the Demands That Float to the Surface

When MIUI has hundreds of thousands of users putting forth ideas on a BBS about what they need, how are you going to rank those needs in order of preference?

What we did inside the company was define product demand in terms of long-term, medium-term, and short-term requirements. Lei Jun would hold meetings with the development team every one to two months to discuss the long-term needs and formulate plans, while the medium- and short-term needs were basically fragmented and handled by the interaction among users. This second process in turn helped inform the revisions of our long-term goals.

In dealing with fragmented demands, we used three methods:

1. **First deal with demand that "floats to the surface."** On the BBS, we used supplementary functions as appropriate, which mainly helped users structure the requests that they were putting forth as much as possible. Then, when users ran into the same needs as others, they could say directly, "I too need that function." At the end of every week, we would discover that the most urgent needs would naturally come to the front of the line. (See Figure 2.4.).

2. **Immediately put out public notices about plans for improvements.** For every week's Orange Friday, the BBS would put out a complete list of functions that had been changed and improved upon from the last week, as well as what had been recommended. In addition, the results of discussions were generally voted on, and those votes

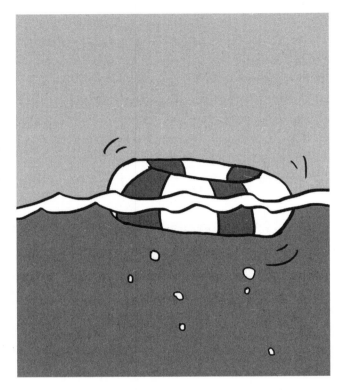

FIGURE 2.4 *First deal with demand that floats to the surface.*

too were put out publicly on the BBS. The team would also put out regular explanations of what the plan for revisions over the coming month was going to be.

3. **Allow the team structure to "fragment" as well.** What this meant was that every two to three people would form a small team, and that team would work on a particular function over a period of time. The teams were given the authority to work on their own, and as they interacted with users, they would decide on and write some 30 percent of the modules in the programming. In the past, it is quite true that we sometimes had engineers who would go off on a wrong track. Surrounded by users as they were, they would develop something that was not in fact all that necessary. However, since the project overall was revised every week, any mistaken plans were not that important because they would be corrected within a week or two.

When I talked to the team about making products, I used the analogy of driving a car. I said, "As long as the overall direction is clear, it doesn't matter if you go off course or slow down a little. The thing you have to worry about is going 180 degrees in the wrong direction, repeatedly, or stopping altogether."

Some projects were not suited to releasing the beta version to the public, in which case, how did we get responses from demand to know how to proceed?

In the initial stage of a start-up, whatever works is what you do. We mobilized employees themselves to do the testing. Following is a story we called the "Big Sales Department."

In July 2010, we decided to do e-commerce ourselves, and four software engineers developed the first version of an e-commerce platform in one month. In order to test this program, we sold cola to our own employees on the e-commerce platform at 90 percent off the regular price. This then was our "Big Sales Department." It used real order forms, and real receipts, and it actually made deliveries (our software engineers themselves "delivered the goods"). Each day it received product and figured its accounts, which allowed us to fix a number of problems in advance of launching the product. By August 29, when the system really went online, all was running smoothly.

The Core Issue of the User Experience Is to Understand the User You Are Designing For

During the first round of fundraising, one evening Lei Jun took me along to meet with the man who became one of our most important investors, the partner in Morningside Ventures named Liu Jin.

We met in a restaurant beside the Fourth Ring Road in Beijing, and we talked until late at night. What most impressed Liu Jin was Xiaomi's innovative model for combining software and hardware and its understanding of the user. While talking away, he suddenly asked us, "What is the user experience?"

At the time, I said that the user had to feel that the product was "good looking and easy to use." Translated into design terminology, we were talking about the user interface/user experience (UI/UE), but the most important requirement in advance of that was to know whom you were designing for.

Determining whom to design for, making it easy to use, and making it good looking—these three things then became an incremental process that gradually defined the user experience.

Many people may in fact overlook the issue of whom they are designing something for, but this needs to be the starting point for designing the user experience (Figure 2.5). Once you determine that, the coordinates for the design system become clear. If you don't have that in mind, you cannot position the product accurately, and you can go way off base since every user group's tastes are different.

For example, you have the group of "elderly people" or "females," both of which require targeted design. One could imagine that older people like neutral gray colors, and not necessarily contrasting primary colors—if you use colors that are too bright, they might find it hard to use the device.

用户体验的核心是为谁设计

FIGURE 2.5 *The core issue of the user experience is to understand the user you are designing for.*

The decision about whom to design for is one that requires input from the product manager, the person in charge of design, and even the CEO. If, however, the CEO is not attuned to this kind of expertise, then designers must take on the responsibility of thinking over all considerations.

Between "good looking" and "easy to use," "easy to use" should always take priority. Our principle is, "Make sure it is easy to use, and just do your best to make it good looking."

This involves choosing among different options. One example could be our function that allows the user to send texts to people with whom he communicates most. The original version, in fact, deleted this function because deleting it made the interface more elegant and simple. We discovered that users really liked this function, however, so the "easy to use" value trumped the "good looking" consideration. We then added the function back in (Figure 2.6).

Another example would be the design of the pull-down notifications, which looked like the squared paper that is used for practicing Chinese calligraphy. From the perspective of the visual experience, deleting it would have made the design better looking, but from user responses we learned that efficiency and "easy to use" came first. So we left in this design element. (See Figures 2.7 through 2.9.).

After satisfying the easy-to-use consideration, our efforts focused on making the product good looking. This process involved two stages. The first was to make attractive features; the second was to give the product a handsome overall style. The second stage was an advance on merely being "good looking" because the design was built into the system and gave it unique elegance. The MIUI design has by now moved into the second stage.

Between 2010 and 2014, MIUI has gone through five versions, and we have consistently tried to improve its looks. Because of this, we came up with the idea of "hundreds of lock screen alternatives and thousands of key-subject alternatives" (Figures 2.10 and 2.11). The good-looking character of the system was a breakthrough that we insisted upon, since the early Android was primitive, and its interface was truly not appealing. We even provided an option of making it highly editable, to beautify it at the deepest levels. We allowed for playing with and interacting with the lock screen.

FIGURE 2.6 *Interface for Writing a New Text Message*

FIGURE 2.7 *Proposal for Showing Contacts When Writing a New Text Message*

FIGURE 2.8 *Interface for Notifications*

FIGURE 2.9 *Proposal for Notifications*

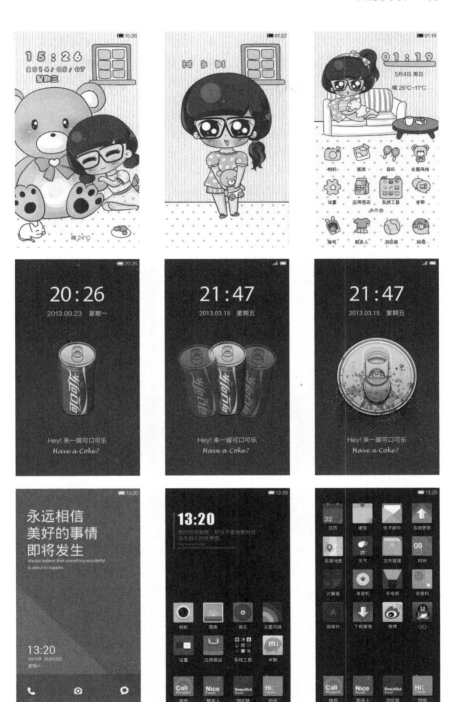

FIGURE 2.10 *Hundreds of Lock Screens on MIUI*

FIGURE 2.11 *Thousand of Key Subjects on MIUI*

With constant improvements as MIUI proceeded through five versions, we began to confirm its overall style and direction. Our own sense of perception, as well as the interactive elements, became more systematic and standardized. We began to feel the thing had more of its own DNA. It had more of a coherent overall design.

The design head of the Japanese company MUJI, Kenya Hara, has said that the starting point for design has to be people, not the product. Only by first considering the person can you design things that feel good when you handle them and that provide a wonderful living environment. The point is to provide things that help people savor the joy of life.

"Whom are you designing for?" This question has to be taken into account when you design, but it is also extremely important at the decision-making level of projects and product management. It can help you find the right sense of rhythm, decide which functions to incorporate and which to leave out, and determine the order of priority of the product. In its first year of development, MIUI put 100 percent of its focus on its fancier groups. At the time, we did not even consider providing firmware installation tools for the public at large. We had only the "development version," not the "stabilized version." Once the number of users went over 10 million, however, user groups became more broadly defined in terms of structure, and we finally began to take different considerations into account and design accordingly.

Turn Activities into Products, and Turn Products into Activities

How does the Xiaomi style of e-commerce gain traffic? In the sales link of the process, how do you foster a sense of engagement? (See Figure 2.12.)

FIGURE 2.12 *Turning Activities into Products, and Turning Products into Activities*

The Xiaomi e-commerce network deals in superlative products—its product strategy is "explosive products." Each of these then becomes an advertisement that pulls in traffic.

Each Tuesday at noon, we hold a sales activity on the Internet. This idea can be considered a first in the whole sphere of e-commerce. We have adhered to this "open-sales" system for each generation of the Mi, from first, to second, to third. Everyone refers to it as Red Tuesday, but behind it is the whole structure of the three-on-three principles of engagement.

Red Tuesday was specifically designed for products that have been on the market just three months or less and that have such strong demand that we cannot supply enough of them. A user first applies online to be qualified to place an advance order for the product. Only users who have placed such advance orders can engage in the "rush-to-purchase" melee of Red Tuesday. Every time we open a sale at 12 noon, traffic suddenly increases on mi.com as millions of users rush in to try to get hold of Mi. This is a boon to our sales staff because they have to do sales only once a week. They can go on holiday the rest of the time. To the backroom staff, however, and the software engineers, the pressure is simply monumental.

Given the intense demand for products and the swift increase in online traffic, the servers were overloaded in the early months of selling smartphones whenever we released a product. Once the servers shut down, moreover, we would be besieged by user complaints. I therefore went to the software engineers and asked if they could make us a custom-made system. Under such intense pressure, they began calling the opening day of product sales Black Tuesday instead of Red Tuesday.

After an immense amount of work, one of our chief engineers improved the programming, but we still did not know whether or not it would stand up to the massive traffic. Prior to the next Red Tuesday, the engineer therefore burned incense and prayed in his office. As it turned out, the system stood up to the test. After that, we rarely had any server problems when we released products. Nevertheless, this custom of burning incense in the engineer's office became a tradition on the day before an opening sale, a kind of gesture to wish the e-commerce department good luck (Figure 2.13).

FIGURE 2.13 *The engineer burns incense prior to the next Red Tuesday.*

We bundled the process of open purchasing together as an "activity" and sold it as a product itself, which involved quite a few details that had to be handled, together with constant improvements, such as keeping automated systems from sweeping up the qualified numbers, and ongoing battles with ticket tout. At the beginning, we just used authentication and verification codes, but later we had users put their smartphone number in as verification before they could proceed to buy. We thereby made it impossible for many automated "water-buffalo systems" to snatch purchasing numbers.

At one point, I presented the planning team with a mission. I asked if they could turn each open-purchasing activity into a topic of conversation on the Internet, a kind of hot subject.

At the outset, users could send us a blog message attached with a photo to declare the success of our product order. This allowed them to declare that they had successfully placed an advance order. In this manner, what had been purely a sales activity also became a social media activity for millions of users. After each Tuesday sale, those who had been able to get hold of Xiaomi products could then share the excitement of that with their friends. Later we added some fun links to the process of making advance orders. For example, people could share which functions they most liked in their Mi, which smartphone cover they thought most represented their own personality, and so on. When placing advance orders for Mi TVs, users could even construct their own digital living room and then choose the color of television set to match. We helped users share images of the results so as to liven up the process of advance ordering and buying via showy blogs.

This was a micro-innovation on the part of Xioami's marketing and sales activities. We turned the product into an activity, and the activity became a way for us to design and make constant improvements to the product.

Xiaomi made other innovative changes to its sales methods, all led by the guiding principle of user engagement. This allowed us to turn what had been one-way purchasing processes into activities that had many different kinds of interaction and engagement. These activities became so stimulating that they became "topics" of conversation, providing their own unique experience.

Each Tuesday's open-sales activity thereby became a major event surrounding consumers' participatory consumption. Each week provided a pulse of social media broadcasting via the Internet. Within this rhythm, Xiaomi itself constantly grew and developed. Previously the cause of intense pressure and headaches, Black Tuesday truly did turn into Red Tuesday for the company.

Everyone who is in the business of e-commerce knows that the trade relies on traffic. Purchasing, pulling in traffic, and return on investment are particularly complex and problematic in this industry. The question for us became whether or not we could guide traffic in ways that were more systematic and predictable. As it turned out, Red Tuesdays were precisely one way to do that. Using them, we could comb through and organize traffic. Naturally, the product first had to be a bestseller, or "explosive." It had to have enough allure to attract people. Given that prerequisite, we channeled the flow of traffic in advance by designing for the process of turning activities into products and by creating attributes that could become topics of conversation.

Corresponding to the idea of turning activities into products is a process I often talk about, that of *turning products into activities*. In making products, you have to use an operational way of thinking—that is, you have to plant things in the design of your products that become functions. Those functions themselves are links in activities.

For example, MIUI is upgraded every week. Two parts of the design of this process are of interest. One is that there is a video lesson teaching the programming at the press conference of each weekly upgrade. After watching that, you can go into a BBS to exchange your own thoughts and ideas. The other is that after the rebooting the upgraded system, we present information that guides users to blogs that allow them to share in and enjoy the newest applications of the new version.

Ultimate Excellence Means You Go Crazy First

How do you make your product the ultimate excellence product?

You definitely do not want to place blind belief in any kind of master or even your own intuition. Both of those point out the "right way to go," but the right direction is just the start. Behind "ultimate" products is an "ultimate" kind of investment, which is hammered out of you yourself. Behind the excellence is a lot of hard work. (See Figure 2.14.)

Here is an example. Redmi 1 was launched with immense success. There were over 7 million advance orders placed via Qzone, but there were only 100,000 phones for sale. Later, Internet fans wondered why the Redmi 1 used the product code H2 instead of H1. In fact, there had been an H1, a first-generation model—but once the engineering version came out, the ease of using the hardware did not meet our required standards. We therefore canceled it altogether and continued our R&D work on the second-generation version. In order to get that "ultimate excellence" experience, we abandoned a first-generation model into which we had put close to RMB 40 million.

Many people are astonished when they first open up the packaging of a Mi (Figure 2.15). It imparts a sense of extremely high quality yet utter simplicity. Many hold onto the boxes as a collector's item. They enjoy the design advances that have been made in the course of Mi 3.

FIGURE 2.14 *Ultimate Excellence Means You Go Crazy First*

A tiny step forward in craftsmanship can become a major advance in terms of the user's experience. In order to ensure that the sides and corners of the carton are absolutely perfect, we had an overseas company custom-make the high-quality craft paper. This ensured greater ease of processing. The selection of materials was just the start. On opening the

FIGURE 2.15 *The Packaging of Mi 3*

cover of the box, you discover that the back of the paper, where it is turned at the corners, has been indented with 12 very fine indentations, so as to ensure that each fold is absolutely straight. The thickness of each piece of craft paper is just a few millimeters. Putting such fine indentations in it shows the care that has gone into making it with ultimate excellence.

In addition to the edges and corners of the packaging, the engineers and designers put tremendous efforts into ensuring its durability as well as ease of use. Once a box is made, it can often expand outward a little, so you have to design it in advance with a slight inclination toward the inside in order to prevent this kind of buckling. Another example: To keep the phone securely held in the box so it won't rattle, and yet make it easy to lift out, the bottom part of the box is one millimeter longer than the top part so it has a stair-stepped kind of impression where you put the phone.

The entire design team worked six months on this box. They went through more than 30 revisions, and they made hundreds of prototypes before having the manufacturer make up 10,000 samples. They finally came up with a box and packaging for the Mi that is truly breathtaking in its quality and craftsmanship. The usual packaging for a smartphone might cost 2 to 3 RMB, but the cost of making a Mi package comes to almost 10 RMB. We believe that the results are well worth the investment.

Let's take a look at the work that goes behind the scripting of one of our press conferences.

Each time a new product is released, we set up a team to do the scripting and design of the presentation. That includes people who do both the writing and the physical design. The team generally includes five people, who work for one and one-half months on the project. Lei Jun participates directly, looking over such major things as the framework of what is to be included as well as such minor things as the color of the written text. It may be hard to believe, but the text can go through as many as a hundred revisions. By the final week prior to a press conference, the people on the team are always crying, I'm going crazy!

At the press conference on April 9, 2013, we worked from 8 p.m. the previous evening until 1 a.m. the next morning. In the half hour before the press conference was to begin, when 80 percent of the attendees were already present, there was a great commotion among the crowd, and it turned out Lei Jun had come in early. He passed through the crowd and came up to the central dais and announced to the designer in charge of the script, "We can move ahead on the basis of what we decided last night, but there are a few places we need to change!"

Ultimate excellence means you have to drive yourself crazy. It means daring to change things. Change, change, change! Then change again!

The Product Is Second; the Team Is First

What is the most important element of a start-up's success?

The most important thing is the team (Figure 2.16). The products come after that because you can make superlative products only if you have a good team.

FIGURE 2.16 *The product is second; the team is first.*

Starting a company is in fact a highly risky thing to decide to do. Behind the few successful start-ups is a field strewn with failures. Many of today's successful companies also had their near-death moments along the way—Alibaba Group is one example. In 1995, Jack Ma led his team in creating China's Yellow Pages, and failed! In 1997, he led them into making a "China product exchange market" on the Internet, the embryonic form of what became Alibaba Group, but that too failed. Alibaba Group has by now become a commercial empire, and people think of it in terms of Taobao, Alipay, and Tmall, but in fact the thing of most value in the company is its team. It is the people behind those names. This particularly means Jack Ma himself and his alliance of 18 cofounders.

In the first year of the company's existence, Lei Jun put the majority of his time into finding the right people.

The most time went into building a team for doing the hardware. When we first started out, most of us came from the Internet industry. We not only did not know much about hardware but we did not have our fingers on the pulse of hardware people. Before meeting one of our cofounders, the man who is now responsible for hardware, Dr. Zhou Guangping, we had already had interviews with other candidates for more than two months. Progress was slow. Some people even had us meet with their "agents" first, to give us their conditions for coming on board. Not only did they want a large number of options but they also wanted even better benefits than what most large companies offer. Sometimes Lei Jun, Lin Bin (a cofounder and vice president of Xiaomi), and I would have follow-up meetings till dawn, at which point we were about to collapse.

The turning point came when Dr. Zhou appeared. According to Lei Jun, he had made up his mind within one hour of talking to him the first time. Later, Dr. Zhou himself told me that he had decided to "join the revolution" within 15 minutes. The "revolution" that he referred to was to make the very best smartphones and to sell them at cost. This was his long-cherished dream.

Dr. Zhou had worked in the hardware side of the smartphone industry for over 20 years. He was globally famous as an expert on signal transmission. Afterward he joined the alliance and created a hardware team. It was as though a light shone in the darkness that brought all of us hope. In the short space of one month, we had settled on 10 more hardware engineers, each of whom had close to 15 years of experience.

In addition, though, we interviewed some candidates who still had doubts about joining this fledgling start-up of a company. What were we to do about them?

Lei Jun and our team of cofounders took turns meeting with them face-to-face. Many times, we got to talking and then found we had talked for nearly 10 hours. The first interview for hiring the person who became responsible for designing the hardware structures of Mi was conducted in Lei Jun's office. The interview started at 1 p.m. By 4, he couldn't hold up any longer and had to take a break by going to the restroom. When he came back, Lei Jun told him that he had asked for a meal to be delivered and they were going to continue talking. They talked until after 11 p.m., when the man finally agreed to join the team. Later he said to me, only half-joking, that he accepted mainly because he had run out of energy.

Four years after Xiaomi was founded, the company's market capitalization came to USD 10 billion. The world looked on this new start-up as a kind of star. That made it even harder for us to find the right people, however, and we had to put massive energy into the process. This was mainly because we insisted on finding people who were not only the most professional but also the most appropriate.

"The most professional" meant not only that they had professional experience in the industry and tremendous capabilities but also that they themselves were able to hire engineers. A single reliable engineer is worth 10 or 100 others. "The most appropriate" meant that the people had to have a "start-up attitude." They had to have an extreme devotion to what they were doing. People with such an attitude are able to ignite themselves. They don't require any external motivation, and you do not need to manage them with a pile of KPI targets and management systems.

I once heard Steve Jobs say something that really moved me. He said, "I used to believe that 1 outstanding person was worth 2 mediocre people. Now I believe 1 is worth 50 other people. I spend roughly one quarter of my time hiring talent." It is said that in his lifetime, Jobs participated in more than 5,000 hiring interviews. In his mind, his core task was to build a first-class team of designers, engineers, and management personnel, an "A team."

Let the Users Excite the Team

A start-up attitude is sometimes referred to as "passion," but how do you keep that passion going in your team?

First, allow the staff to become Mi Fans (Figure 2.17). Whenever new employees start work at Xiaomi, they get a Mi that is the main phone for their daily use. In addition, they get the ability to invite their friends to be users. Every month, every Xiaomi employee can provide a certain number of friends or family with F Code, which refers to Friend Code. These codes provide the friend with preferential purchasing qualifications. Finally, we ask each new employee to become "friends" with users.

FIGURE 2.17 *Let the users excite the team.*

Many traditional companies are opposed to having friends use their own products for free. As the saying goes, "The fox preys farthest from home." In Xiaomi, we have a different saying, which is, "We would even let our mother-in-law use our products!"

I realize that a lot of companies prevent their R&D department from having any contact with the outside world. Instead, when MIUI was just getting started, I encouraged engineers to cultivate contacts with users through the BBS. At the beginning, some highly qualified engineers considered this somewhat unthinkable—they generally had 5 or 10 years of experience, and they thought it was more cost effective for them to sit and peacefully write code for an hour. They shouldn't be asked to waste time talking to users. Their rationale was, "Why not ask the customer service people in Xiaomi to do the customer interaction?"

I told them, "We do it differently in Xiaomi. If you don't understand, we'll just put it in as part of your performance evaluation."

In Xiaomi, surfing the BBS is indeed part of work. If people are not too busy, they can spend an hour at it, but if they are busy, 15 minutes will suffice. At first, this requirement was implemented on a mandatory basis, every day. During that initial period, we regarded this as being on the same level of importance as debugging systems. Issues that showed up in responses from users were listed in the "task list" of our internal development group. Only once we had built this platform and we had made sure the entire team had gotten on board could we feel we had really taken hold of what the users needed. Only then were we really focused on the users, and only then were our first-line product managers and development teams focused on the users. Developers were no longer just working from cold statistical tables. Users, meanwhile, were no longer just facing a monotonous record of revisions.

The fond feelings that Xiaomi people have for their own products are similar to many people's feelings about their children. Here are two stories about Lei Jun in that regard.

In May 2011, the first test call of the Mi 1 was just coming in. At that point, it was just an electric circuit board sitting on a table. We happened to be having a meeting in nearby offices that day. When the engineer said the call was happening, Lei Jun was first to charge out the door, without even excusing himself. He bent down trying to hear the sound. Since it was so weak, he put one ear to it, and then the other, and almost crouched on top of the table itself to hear the connection (Figure 2.18).

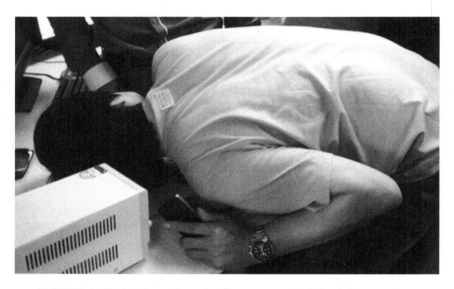

FIGURE 2.18 *In May 2011, the first test call of the Mi 1 was just coming in. He bent down trying to hear the sound. Since it was so weak, he put one ear to it, and then the other, and almost crouched on top of the table itself to hear the connection.*

When Mi 1 came out, people had massive doubts about the quality of China-made smart phones. They couldn't believe Chinese manufacturers used the certified materials. Whenever a journalist raised such doubts at small-scale meetings with the press, Lei Jun would stop everything, no matter what was scheduled on down the line for the meeting, to talk about this. He would patiently explain to everyone that our parts were supplied by world-class suppliers and that we were using an assembly plant that had previously been used by Apple. He would talk himself up into such a state that he would even demonstrate how our smartphone was unbreakable. To symbolize how our quality was up to anything, he'd throw one on the ground and not just once, but two or three times.

Here's another story about the pressures of those early days.

In October 2011, when the Mi was just beginning to be sold, our production capacity was also just getting up to speed, and we could produce only 500 phones a day, 1,000 at the outside. More than 300,000 people had signed up for the very first "advance purchase" of the phones, however. This multiplied the pressures on us. Xiaomi was a beginner when it came to everything from production to logistics, from customer service to post-sales follow-up, and we had only slightly more than a hundred people at the time. We worked like mad all day long in order to get the production numbers up.

One day, at 2 a.m., I was driving home, and I began to feel the pressure was just too much. So I stopped by the side of the road and just stayed quiet for a while. The reason was that we were supposed to deliver product this day, but Thailand had floods and the batteries for the phones had been delayed. This meant we were unable to keep our promise. The Xiaomi BBSs were covered with scathing complaints from users.

Suddenly, I got a private message on Weibo—it was from Leo, one of our earliest users. He said he had something to give us, and he hoped it would help Xiaomi hold on. It was a brief video sent out on the Xiaomi BBS—users from all over the country were shouting out the words: Xiaomi, come on!

In that moment, the tears came streaming down.

Even more moving were the small gifts that regular users sent us from around the country. At the beginning, I put these on the table in our office, but then I had to build a cabinet to display them as they increased. By now, the display cabinets cover two walls.

When I show people a "phone" that is really made from millet, I generally make the comment that all the tens of millions of phones we have made are "copycat" compared to this one. The reason is that this "phone" is made from real millet by one of our users (Figure 2.19).

FIGURE 2.19 *A Phone That Is Really Made from Millet*

It is hard to imagine that an ordinary consumer would take the trouble to make such a gift with his own hands and send it to the company that had sold him a product. The relationship between Xiaomi and its users is not just that of buyer and seller. Instead, users are deeply engaged in the process of "growing" together with Xiaomi. They have established a deep-seated emotional attachment with us.

CHAPTER 3

BRAND

What Do They Think?

It's not a matter of implanting our thought into the consumers' consciousness. It is a matter of infiltrating consumers' consciousness to obtain their thought.

"Who am I?"

The first question that has to be answered when you are creating a brand is that of identity—that is, how you position your product.

The classic theory of "positioning" talks about developing and channeling the growth of a whole new product category. It involves figuring out how to differentiate your product in the minds of potential users. The triumph of Xiaomi has, first and foremost, been the triumph of creating a new product category called the "Internet smartphone."

What justifies this as being a new category? The thing people can actually see and understand mainly relates to how the phone uses the Internet, how it is sold via the Internet, and how it uses e-commerce. In fact, however, behind all of this is the fact that the very form of the product has been altered because the phone's systems are "alive." They are regenerated weekly, based on user opinions. Second, the business model has also changed. We have consistently adhered to the idea that hardware will be sold at cost in the future. How does that affect the business model? Profits come from selling the application services of the mobile Internet as opposed to selling the phones themselves. The new product category of this Internet smartphone is therefore different in all respects, from the form that "the product" itself takes, to the way it is sold, to the entire business model behind it.

All of the products that Xiaomi decides to make must first take into consideration the logic behind that product's category. The reason is that when users buy something, they first subconsciously choose a product category and then they choose a brand within that category. The Mi invented a new product category: the Internet smartphone. The Mi TV also invented a new product category: the "first TV" that young people buy in their lives.

When we started making Redmi, we also initiated a core category: the 1,000 RMB phone. In strategic terms, we had a very clearly defined idea of what the Redmi should be—it was supplementary to the 2,000 RMB Mi, in order to open up the 1,000 RMB market. In the China market, there are only two grades of smartphones, those under and those over 1,000 RMB. The 1,000 RMB phone is basically a fixed concept, a product category. The price of 1,999 RMB is a unique price point that Xiaomi opened up in the market, through differentiating itself.

In "killer" categories in other spheres, other companies also do meticulous research into the language to be used for promotion. This is not a simple matter of selling but rather of educating the public more thoroughly about the product category. Red Bull is an example. Red Bull is selling a function, not just a drink: "Thirsty? Drink Red Bull. Tired, sleepy—even more reason to drink Red Bull." The ice tea Jia Duo Bao is another example: "Don't want to suffer from excessive internal heat? Then drink Jia Duo Bao." Yunnan Baiyao is another example: "With a better medicine, you could be cured faster."

In today's Internet age, the ways of positioning a product are still as they have been, in terms of focusing on user group aggregates and simplifying how those groups transmit information. Nevertheless, I believe there are also two major differences:

1. Previously, companies had a "competitive mentality" whereas now the mentality is more about the product itself.
2. Previously, the idea was to implant our thought into the consumers' consciousness, whereas now it is to infiltrate the consumers' consciousness to obtain their thought (Figure 3.1).

In doing preliminary analysis, competing is a useful tool, but it becomes counterproductive as time goes on and as you develop the

FIGURE 3.1 *It's not a matter of implanting our thought into the consumers' consciousness. It is a matter of infiltrating the consumers' consciousness to obtain their thought.*

product. The reason is that it forces you to focus on the opponent and not your users. A "product mentality" in Internet terms talks about such things as focus, ultimate excellence, word-of-mouth reputation, and speed. What you are focusing on is the value being created by the product, making it "ultimate excellence." Meanwhile, the classic way we implanted our thought into the consumers' consciousness was to try to educate people through brainwashing. This involved ruthlessly repetitive advertising over a long period of time. In contrast, infiltrating consumers' consciousness is a matter of our being recommended by word-of-mouth reputation, of inviting users themselves into the process.

The most extreme example of the kind of implanting thought into the consumers' consciousness is the method used by the health supplements industry. This industry constantly "teaches" you how supplements are good for you without actually divulging the product behind the message. In contrast, the kind of branding that penetrates users' minds without using advertising is a kind that uses word-of-mouth reputation to seep into awareness. In the process of actual usage, the users themselves are constantly making innovations in the products and services.

An example is the company JD.com, which now has a market capitalization of USD 30 billion. In the early period, its founder, Liu Qiangdong, started with just one counter in the Zhongguancun Science Park. He was the very first to openly declare prices on his products. In that early period, he almost went under because he had no money, no sales channels, and no customers. However, three months later, customers began spreading the word about his products, which generated tremendous prestige value, and he increased his size to four counters. He went on from there. This mode of infiltrating consumers' consciousness takes a long time, but it has much greater force.

By what path was the brand able to enter into people's awareness? With both MIUI and the company's smartphone, the path made use of user groups as the core radial influence in a constantly broadening circle. The brand first infiltrated the awareness of professional users, then went on from there as it was transmitted, layer by layer. Product functionality used the same mode of infiltration. For example, the first thing people sensed about MIUI was its ease of use and its speed. After that, they realized it was also good looking, and after that they came to realize that it had a lot of functions that could automatically distinguish what to do, such as free Wi-Fi when you entered Wi-Fi hot spots. Users found it easier and easier to use as they personalized their own systems. A countless number of micro-innovations in functionality gave users a sense of satisfaction. These constantly worked their way into the users' mind, to the extent that people really became "addicted" after using the MIUI system for a while. It became uncomfortable to try to use other systems. This kind of infiltrating consumers' consciousness is more powerful than implanting thought into consumers' consciousness.

Many of the innovative strategies we use today came about because we had no alternative. In 2010, when we had just launched the start-up, we did some research into two brands that were hot at the time.

One was a fast fashion company called VANCL:

1. This company focused its media resources by only investing in bill-board advertising. What's more, it saturated the market and achieved complete penetration as a result. Using a limited amount of money, it was able to gain maximum results.
2. As a new brand on the Internet, it used "spokespeople" to push the product. For the next generation, it found the hottest possible idol for that demographic sector. For the mass market, it promoted the idea of positive energy, through such superstars as Li Yuchun.
3. VANCL put prices directly on its ads—something that the other companies rarely did at that time. In fact, it used inexpensive t-shirts (29 RMB) and canvas (69 RMB) shoes as the actual items being advertised, as it spread brand awareness.

Another was a company that made a China-produced music phone:

1. This company used media resources in an extremely clever way. It named almost all the famous music and entertainment programmers on TV.
2. Its "star strategy' involved using superstars but not idols. For example, using the international superstar Leonardo DiCaprio as a spokesperson was very successful.
3. The packaging of the brand was meticulously and beautifully done. Many people thought this was a South Korean or French brand because the name of the company and its design features followed a Japanese, South Korean, or international model. Nevertheless, its main sales channels were concentrated in second- and third-tier cities, which was a highly intelligent approach.

In June 2011, we began trying to find someone to be the head of marketing for Mi. Lei Jun and I met with a number of people who generally would say to us, "You should do advertising," or "You should open a chain of physical stores." This was disappointing since Xiaomi wanted to find someone who not only could sell but someone who also could truly understood the concept of an Internet smartphone.

After two months, when we still had not found the right person, Lei Jun came to me and asked me to take on the challenge.

At the outset, we put together a marketing plan that was going to cost RMB 30 million. We thought we would use the media plan adopted by VANCL and put billboards throughout the country at major points, for a month. Lei Jun rejected this plan on the spot. He said, "Alee, when you did MIUI, you did not spend a penny. Can't you do the same thing with the smartphone? Can't we continue to open up the market without spending money?"

At the time, my first reaction was to think that MIUI was a system, and users could use it without spending money. Marketing the smartphone was different because users had to spend money to buy one. The question in my mind was therefore this: A smartphone is an actual thing that costs RMB 2,000. If you don't put any money into advertising at all, is it really realistic to think that users will spring for that bill?

Xiaomi was a totally new brand, plus it had no money, no "matchmakers," and no resources for advertising. With no alternatives, we had to do everything we could to use social media.

What we did was to think of ways that used BBSs and microblogging. We started by selecting BBSs with which we were familiar. The great advantage here was that we could sift out our "old users" and have them help us. However, this was going to be slow in terms of radiating out influence to user groups. At that time, microblogging had just begun to be popular. These blogs served as excellent supplements to the BBS. We started doing considerable research into how to "play" with microblogs, and we found a pathway to establishing a brand on Internet.

Each person has a unique style and a unique voice. Each brand also has its own distinctive voice. On today's Internet, users are highly attuned to the authenticity of that voice, to the authenticity of the brand.

Many brands do not make the cut in terms of being broadly disseminated, and the reasons are simple:

1. When answering the question "Who am I," that is, talking about their "identity," they exaggerate themselves in highpoint terms.
2. They try to become famous before establishing credibility and trustworthiness. Before the number of users has reached a certain scale, and before the company has established a good foundation in response to the question "Who am I," they set up strange cross-brand cooperative arrangements and promote so-called star strategies, all of which look false and empty. Instead, you must first establish loyal followers.

Loyalty Versus Popularity

Does Xiaomi have some exclusive tips?

Xiaomi has taken a different path to brand development. This is directly related to our understanding of our business model and recent changes in consumer demand.

The age when people merely consumed the direct function of a thing was an age in China that had no brands at all. Once we entered a brand age, the brands belonged to companies. Now, however, what we need to establish are brands that belong to users. That means inviting the users in, engaging the users.

Generally speaking, the route to establishing a brand in traditional industries was that you first established popularity, then you aimed for reputation, and finally you aimed for loyalty. In the Internet age, the product is the brand. Often, therefore, you first aim for reputation, and then you aim for popularity. When you are emphasizing the value of functionality in Internet products, however, it is fundamentally very hard to set up loyalty.

Our branding method has therefore dealt with this differently. From the start, we focused solely on loyalty, including credibility and trustworthiness. Through word-of-mouth reputation, we constantly strengthened this process until we had enough volume. Only then did we put any investment into establishing popularity (Figure 3.2).

FIGURE 3.2 *Loyalty is primary; popularity is secondary.*

MIUI started out with just a user base of 100 people. Through word-of-mouth, that broadened out until today we have a user base that numbers over 60 million people. In the early period of accumulating users, we focused especially on accumulating loyalty at the same time. We therefore focused on the "purity" of those users. At the time, one of our colleagues recommended that we put out firmware installation software that used only MIUI. I rejected this idea. It was not in line with getting ever more users to use the system. Instead, we needed to focus on calling together fan users, so as to preserve the purity of the "seed stock" of our initial users. If too many fresh users came in too soon, the ability of the core user group of MIUI to recommend it would be compromised.

In thinking about brands, popularity means that you have the ability to make a user sit up and pay attention. Reputation means that you have the ability to reach users. In contrast to these, loyalty means that you are inside the minds of users. A so-called Mi Fans culture depends on having a number of loyal users.

The company called Beats Electronics, which makes high-end headphones, was purchased by Apple for the sum of USD 3 billion. One reason I like this brand is that it became the number one brand in high-end headphones, outselling Sony, Bose, and other major traditional brand names, and the most important reason for that success was its fan culture. Its founder was an American, Dr. Dre, who used quite courageous methods to generate acceptance and to inculcate a sense of engagement among users.

Xiaomi has always worked hard to cultivate fan users. By providing them with the feeling that they are participating in the process, we keep them liking us to the point that they become friends. Only after gaining a sufficient loyalty do we begin to expand promotion via traditional sales methods and spending on ads. In 2013 and 2014, Xiaomi began advertising in conjunction with the Spring Festival Gala, and it increased its advertising campaign, and it promoted its brand image step by step, basing the promotions on our thousands of fan users.

A sense of engagement is the very soul of the brand mind. I believe that what young people are actually consuming is this feeling of engagement. They are not just buying what they can see and feel, but rather, something they can join into, by which they can grow as well.

Some people feel that Xiaomi users are a bit crazy. In fact, people have no idea of the true nature of the relationship between our team and our users—they don't realize that the extent of the engagement is far beyond what they can imagine. Even today, we do our utmost not to put out ads. We would like to extend the model that we started out with from the beginning. That forces us to consider how we can get users to like our products voluntarily, on their own initiative, how we can make the experience and aesthetic appeal of our products enter into the very minds of our users.

The Fans Effect

So how does Xiaomi create this fans effect?

"If pigs stand at the right place in the typhoon, they can indeed fly." This vivid saying is Lei Jun's way of "going with the flow," which means aligning yourself with the forces around you. He has unwavering

FIGURE 3.3 *The fans effect is what can make pigs fly.*

confidence in this idea of positive alignment in how he manages affairs. In 2010, he named the investment fund that he set up Shunwei, which means "going with the flow." If you think of the founder of a start-up as a "lucky pig," the overall conditions of the industry are the "typhoon" that lifts the pig, and those overall conditions include the engagement of users (Figure 3.3).

In 2013, we created an online micro-movie as part of the annual meeting, and we called it *Benefactors of One Hundred Dreams* (Figures 3.4 and 3.5). It told the story of a young person in a small town who held onto his dream. The original form of this story came from the actual situation that existed when Xiaomi was just starting out. When

FIGURE 3.4 *The First Internal-Trial Version of MIUI*

FIGURE 3.5 *Benefactors of One Hundred Dreams*

we put out the first internal-trial version of MIUI, there were only 100 users. The company was unknown at the time, and it had done no promotion whatsoever, so this initial 100 names became highly precious "seed stock." We called them our "benefactors of one hundred dreams." When the official version of MIUI was released, in order to express our appreciation to these people, we had the BBS IDs of the 100 names listed on the opening screen when the system started up.

These 100 names were also printed on the side of the racecar in our movie, which represented the dream of this particular young person. The movie was meant to be an expression of how we appreciated and respected these users, but it also became a classic in the minds of all user groups and Xiaomi employees.

Through the word-of-mouth recommendations of the first 100 benefactors, each new revision of the program every week resulted in multiples of that number in new users. The initial group proved Xiaomi's hypothesis: word-of-mouth reputation is a powerful force behind creating good products. By June 2014, the number of people using MIUI came to over 60 million.

Long before Mi 1 came out, what we later came to call Mi Fans user groups were already appearing. These people were extremely keen on MIUI in user BBSs, and at the beginning we called them by various names. Some of us called them "mi-you," which means "Mi friends," using the same sound as MIUI. Some of us called them "mi-fan," but gradually we all standardized on the term "Mi Fans." In general, it refers to the most active group of Xiaomi users. These are the ones who engage in the R&D process of creating Xiaomi products, and they are also the key links in crafting its brand. In July 2011, at the very first press conference, when we were revealing that Xiaomi was going to put out a "fancier smartphone," we said that we believed good products could speak for themselves. Users would recommend them to one another (Figure 3.6). Many people did not believe that Xiaomi could succeed with this strategy, but it was in fact the approval and support of each and every user that is what

FIGURE 3.6 *Mi Products Selected by Mi Fans*

propelled us forward. We therefore have a saying within the company, "Xiaomi gets success thanks to Mi Fans." It means customers leading products.

I believe that you cannot design a "fans effect." This is one manifestation of the theory of out of control that the Internet philosopher Kevin Kelly talked about in his book *Out of Control*.

Ultimately, the subconscious nature of group consciousness unwittingly chooses a mode of behavior that is most suited to that group. This in fact comes up with an expression of maximized results.

Once the economic effect of this fans effect began to be apparent, some companies recognized its value, but they did precisely the opposite of what was required. They intentionally tried to design a fans effect into their plans even before they began interacting with users. This had the unintended consequence of making users lose the most important thing—namely, that crucial sense of engagement. Since engagement was being externally planned, it did not come from within.

The fans effect starts with just a small "tribe." People come together as the result of a common interest. The decentralized nature of the Internet will in the future generate countless numbers of such differentiated tribes.

Xiaomi first created the MIUI software system and then later released the smartphone hardware. Both hardware and software adhered to the philosophy of "being born for the sake of fans." The high functionality of the phones and the way users could custom-make their own versions and play with the software were both highly unique features that attracted many fancier users. The first 100 benefactors of MIUI were the starting points of the users, and the 500,000 users the hardware, the seed stock of the company. Meanwhile, the active participants in Xiaomi BBSs have been the starting point, the point of origin, for the company's tens of millions of users.

The fans effect cannot be designed, but it can be guided depending on circumstances, in order to provide it with a greater sense of interactivity and engagement.

We provide that sense of engagement in a number of ways, including revising MIUI every Orange Friday depending on users' opinions. We provide it via open purchasing via the Xiaomi network (mi.com) on Red Tuesdays and also via offline activities such as MIPOP and the Mi Fans Festival held every year.

The Mi Fans Festival started in April 2012, when the company was reaching its second anniversary and wanted to do something to celebrate (Figure 3.7). Lei Jun and I both felt that the core factor contributing to the success of Xiaomi had been the support of its Mi Fans, so we defined each annual celebration as a Mi Fans Festival as a kind of payback to users and also to celebrate together with users.

On June 7, 2014, we were going to hold the annual offline activity called MIPOP. As usual, on June 6, some of our colleagues planned to

FIGURE 3.7 *The First Mi Fans Festival in 2012*

fly down to that year's location of the event, Zhuhai, in southern China, to set up the event hall. Who could have known that a typhoon would hit that day, delaying all flights. In a panic, we thought of switching flights to get first to Shenzhen or Guangzhou and then on to Zhuhai. By the time our colleagues reached Zhuhai, it was already 1 a.m. on the morning of the seventh, but in fact the meeting place had already been set up in advance by a dedicated group of Mi Fans supporters. The heroes behind the scene were around a dozen local Zhuhai people. As we were sitting around waiting for the plane, these people had handled all the arrangements through instructions over the telephone from some 2,200 kilometers away.

Such is the force of fans power. That kind of support really moved us, and it also reminded us that we truly are lucky pigs.

Users as Stars

How do you ignite a sense of engagement offline?

Our MIPOP is an offline activity. In fact, it is a chance for users to meet one another. The company has a system of puffed rice activities that includes dozens of meetings every year, as well as more than 500 spontaneous gatherings put together by users themselves in various cities. Activities also include the annual MIPOP Gala at the end of every year.

The first time we did a MIPOP activity was in September 2011. The Mi had not been out in the public eye for even a month, and it was fairly unknown. We therefore held two consecutive MIPOP events for users, one in Shanghai and one in Guangzhou. We were astonished by the enthusiasm of users in Shanghai; we had rented a space that could accommodate 200 people. As it happened, nearly 400 people squeezed into the place. Not only were there Mi Fans from Shanghai but there were also aficionados from all the surrounding areas including Suzhou and Wuxi.

The original idea behind MIPOP events came from car clubs. When people want to buy a car, they often surf car-talk BBSs on the Internet, and they also get together offline for eating and drinking. When I myself was buying my first car, I surfed the car BBSs for two months and then discovered that friends and colleagues in Xiaomi were doing the same thing. They would surf the auto.sohu.com and the xcar.com.cn to see who was recommending what, in order to choose the best option for themselves. After doing this for a while, people remained "car friends" even after they had purchased their car. People tended to trust their car friends and believe their word-of-mouth recommendations.

Later, I discovered that users were behaving in a similar fashion when they purchased Mi. They would make several comparisons with other companies' smartphones, look over the accessories, and also see what other people were saying. When fans bought a smartphone, they would dissect all the various parameters and compare them with other brands. How big was the display? Was it 4.5 inches, or was it 4.7 inches? Was the CPU a dual-core processor or a quad-core processer? Was the CPU frequency 1.5 gigahertz, or was it 1.7? How about the power consumption? And the battery—did it last 2,000 milliamps or 3,000? Their understanding of these things went far beyond what most people imagine.

In fact, more users bought a particular smartphone on the basis of recommendations than on anything else—it was the final thing influencing their purchasing decision. A lot of our users would recommend a Mi to family and colleagues in an office, as well as to their friends. As a result, an entire office or an entire family would end up using the same model. For example, 30 percent of the users of our Redmi are purchased by family members to give to either parents or children.

To many fanciers, a Mi is not merely a small device with which they can make phone calls or send text messages, or on which they can install various apps. Instead, the phone is something with which they can have fun. It has many aspects that make it attractive to a group of people who can share features and mutually shine as a result (Figure 3.8). We wondered, therefore, if we could emulate the car club model and make a platform that allowed user s who enjoyed playing with their smartphone to get together and commune with one another. That is why we started the MIPOP.

The MIPOP event is not a road show. We do not conduct any promotion or advertising or put out product displays. Instead, it is simply a way for everyone to get together and play. It is a stage on which users can exhibit themselves and where they can meet new friends.

FIGURE 3.8 *Each user is a star.*

As with the three-on-three principles for creating a sense of engagement, the entire process of the MIPOP event is open to user engagement. Users may vote to decide which city the next one will be held in. Furthermore, the program includes events in which users themselves perform—those performing are selected in advance via the BBSs. Mi Fans volunteer do the setting up of the hall. At the conclusion of each MIPOP event, the most experienced local Mi Fans will get together afterward with our team for dinner and conversation.

Starting in 2011, toward the end of each year we organize what we call the Annual MIPOP Gala (Figure 3.9). We invite the Mi Fans who have grown together with us over the year to come to Beijing from all over the country. All of the founders attend this banquet-like event, as well as the heads of departments. People take photographs together, play games, and enjoy themselves, and they also get to eat specially prepared, fragrant, delicious popcorn!

The peak state of a sense of engagement is the feeling of becoming a star.

We roll out a red carpet at these annual events, and we set up a T-shaped dance floor. Through communities, our several million Mi Fans select several dozen to attend, who are highly qualified in different areas. We film them walking down the red carpet as each one goes up to receive his own "golden Mitu award." Mitu is a plush toy designed by Xiaomi, and it looks like a rabbit. As it happens, Mi Fans begin to discover that they have big-name stars among them. At one time, these big names were, just like all the rest, participants in Xiaomi BBSs, on Weibo, or within their own Group Chats. In the course of other MIPOP activities, through engagement, they started to be pushed to the forefront as the most stellar of all. In addition to these things, we also put out a MIPOP magazine, and Mi Fans become cover girls (Figure 3.10).

All of this, in fact, represents the greatest difference between Xiaomi and traditional brands: we actually play with our users. Whether online or offline, at any given time we are always trying to think of ways to enable our users to "come on in," to feel like they are part of the Xiaomi team.

FIGURE 3.9 *The Annual MIPOP Gala*

FIGURE 3.10 *The MIPOP Magazine and the Activity*

We want them to feel that they are the stars behind making the products better, and behind promoting the brand.

Not Losing the Race at the Starting Line

The first step in creating a start-up company is confirming what your product is and how it is going to solve the sore point. Only then do you begin to think about the company name, its domain name, its branding motto, its mascot, and so on. We put a great deal of time and effort into these things once we decided to launch the brand. I used to say, only half-jokingly, that we did not want to lose the race right at the starting line (Figure 3.11).

Three-in-One

Thinking up a good name for a company is not at all an easy thing to do. Our main considerations included the following:

1. In Chinese, it had to be memorable and easy to transmit or pass along to others.
2. It had to be able to get hold of the highest-level domain names for accompanying products.
3. It had to be a name we could register as a trademark.
4. It had to be easily rolled out internationally.
5. It had to something familiar, yet colorful and full of emotional appeal.

In the first month of the start-up's existence, the founding team must have discussed more than a hundred possible names. They included things like Red Star, Qianqi, Antong, Xuande, and Lingxi. Looking back on it now, some of these were amusing, and some were merely trying to be novel. Lingxi was one example—we wanted to use the idea behind a particular phrase in Chinese: "The heart has an opening to the outside world that is as slender as the single-thread conduit in a rhinoceros horn." We even went as far as designing a rhinoceros mascot on paper. Xuande was another example. Meaning "profound

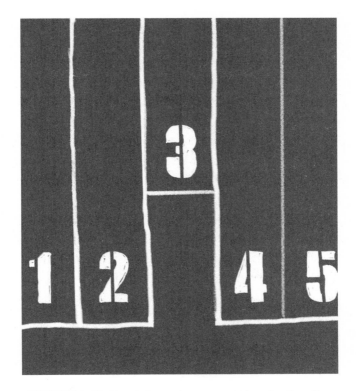

FIGURE 3.11 *Don't lose the race at the starting line when creating a brand.*

virtue," it also was the name on the boxes from the restaurant in which we had our earliest discussions.

We almost settled on the name Red Star at one point. It would be easily recognized, and the idea of a shimmering red star seemed to have a lot of positive energy and excitement. The owner of the top-tier domain name had even named a price to us, but it turned out that since Red Star was also the name of a famous kind of alcohol, it was subject to special protection. Even though it was in the "technology category" of commercially registered names, its sale was prohibited.

In the end, we chose Xiaomi. *Xiaomi* means "millet" in Chinese, one of the five grains. Not only is it lustrous and nourishing but it is also something familiar to people, something that gives them a sense of familiarity and commonality. Everyone knows the term *millet*. When I went to register it at the Bureau of Industry and Commerce, I was asked if I was setting up a new agricultural technology company.

The design of the graphic for the logo uses the first two letters of the words *mobile Internet*: MI. These also spell the way to pronounce the Chinese word for "millet." If you turn the graphic 180 degrees, it also looks similar to the Chinese character for *heart*: 心 if you add just one little dot. It means let the product be easy for the customer to use.

Having a simple and familiar name is conducive to gathering in the greatest amount of traffic, as is having a simple domain name such as xiaomi.com. Some very familiar brands did not put sufficient effort into thinking about their names in the early period. They failed to make sure that their company name, their logo, and their domain name all conformed to the principle of three-in-one—so they failed to optimize the best possible combination. This means that they lose traffic when search engines sift through data and when daily information is transmitted.

Experience tells us that you should do your best to avoid using a name like "The Age of XX," or "XX Wireless." These require the addition of auxiliary words, which slows things down. After setting up the company, we decided to put every effort into registering the name Xiaomi Technology and into ensuring that we could get the domain name. If we could not get that domain name, we would not go any further.

Xiaomi officially launched its business into international markets in 2014. In order to do that, we did not hesitate to put money into buying the domain name mi.com. When we purchased the domain name xiaomi.com, we only spent a few hundred thousand RMB. To buy mi.com, we were required to put out USD 3.6 million in real money. The advantage was that mi.com was appropriate to international promotion—this domain name made it much easier to spread the concept of "mobile Internet" on a global basis.

Born for Fans

Xiaomi has consistently adhered to the branding strategy that declares the company is "born for fans." This applied to its earliest product project: MIUI. Later it was extended to smartphones, and then to routers and to all of the hardware and software products. Xiaomi itself was established by a group of people who "love to play" and who are themselves fanciers, or hot-headed enthusiasts. Both Lei Jun and I, as well as the other founders, are digital fanciers. Before deciding to make a fancier's smartphone, we had already decided that, no matter what size the market might be, we would stick to this founding principle. We would make a group of things that we ourselves liked and we would make the kind of smartphone that only fanciers like us would like.

Put in the most direct and honest terms, "born for fans" means that the whole idea is to play. I often explain the differences between Mi smartphones and other smartphones in this way: users of other brands "use" their phones. The users of Mi "play with" their phones. Moreover, you don't just have one person playing—you have people getting together to play. That's why you see users with their phones playing with installing systems, running remote control cars, using them for delayed-action photographs, even photographing the moon. Xiaomi users often get to know each other on BBSs because they use the same phone, and they then get together for offline meetings if they are in the same city.

The prerequisite for the success of any start-up product is that the product must first satisfy the founders' requirements. If they themselves are not truly satisfied, how can the product hope to move someone else? Companies in any industry that are "ultimate," that turn the industry upside down, have this feature in common. Not long ago, I was talking with Wang Wei, who is the founder of S.F. Express. He said that he started his business 20 years ago precisely because he was not satisfied with delivery services at the time and he decided that he would simply "do it himself." He would make a better service.

The best branding declarations or mission statements are simple and succinct. They express one's own hopes and aspirations, and they thereby stimulate other people to want the same things. For example, Google's mission statement has been, "To organize the world's information and make it universally accessible and useful." Alibaba Group's statement is, "Making it easy to do business anywhere in the world." As for purity, I once said that people who "live for the fever" are different from most others. They dare to be themselves. Without being too fastidious, they are highly driven, and they believe anything is possible. Look at the mottos:

"Make information universally accessible and useful," "Make it easy to do business anywhere in the world," "For China Dream, just do it!"

In the four years since it was founded, Xiaomi's user base has gone from fans to a more general market. We are therefore repositioning the branding and the company's mission. Instead of "Born to serve the fans," we want to indicate that Xiaomi is making products with the end user in mind, that by using an Internet mode of selling, we can eliminate intermediaries and sell globally via e-commerce. We have not yet wrapped this up in a succinct statement, but the idea is that it should be possible for everyone to purchase good products. "Born to serve fans" continues to be a product strategy because it incorporates the idea of high functionality, high ability to custom design yourself, and high usability. These features encapsulate the Xiaomi brand (Figure 3.12).

Mascot: Mitu

A mascot is a way to express the overall perception of a brand (Figure 3.13). Not all brands require a mascot of course, but for mass-market brands, a mascot helps soften the image of a company and make it more approachable in terms of communicating with users.

The Mitu is our mascot, our "auspicious animal" (Figure 3.14). After deciding on the name of Xiaomi, we began to consider the idea of a mascot because we felt that it would help the overall image of an impersonal Internet company become more "warm and fuzzy." Thinking about what the mascot should be therefore began on the day the company was founded, together with the company name and its logo. People ask why we chose a rabbit... Well, the reason is actually because there are not that many animals available that fit the purpose.

We had three possible candidates in deciding on this issue.

The first was a "primitive man," a caveman. "Born for fans" meant that Xiaomi was a mobile Internet company that produced products with high functionality, and the stronger the "tech" feel to the company, the more it was in conflict with traditional kinds of mascots. We wanted to show we were the kind of company that turned the world upside down. Nevertheless, the image that was designed was not comprehensible to a niche market, so it was rejected.

FIGURE 3.12 *The Distinctive Look of Xiaomi*

FIGURE 3.13 *Mascot Alternatives*

FIGURE 3.14 *Mitu*

The second was a small dinosaur. This was a baby dinosaur that was arrogant usually and had much explosive power when it was angry. We drew up a number of adorable little dinosaurs, but in the end Lei Jun rejected the whole idea. Dinosaurs are extinct, he pointed out. The implications are therefore not so great.

The third was a rabbit, what we call the Mitu.

The Mitu, which is Aries, is drawn in a way to express enthusiasm and delight in new and curious things. It is adorable, and it takes pleasure in exploring the world with companions. It has a calm exterior with staring eyes, but behind its eyes are countless new ways of thinking. In the simplest terms, Mitu doesn't put on any airs but is still a little unusual.

In 2013, Xiaomi sold more than RMB 1 billion in peripheral products. Within this figure were sales of 500,000 Mitu toys (Figure 3.15). On April 8, 2014, the company had a Mi Fans Festival. On that day alone, it sold over 170,000 Mi-bunnies. Sales are expected to continue to grow.

FIGURE 3.15 *Mitu Toys*

Basic Source Material as the Lifeline of
Broadcasting Power, or Transmission

When each new product is released, putting all the presentation together for the press conference and getting the product site ready is just half of the process.

This is pretty much the opposite of the way many large companies approach the subject. We have had dealings with some of the American Association of Advertising Agencies (4A advertising companies). In defining a new product and getting it ready for release, they generally put tremendous effort into the "big concept," and a sense of "form." Some companies even recommend not doing any kind of product website at all because they think users won't look at it and won't understand it if they do. They feel that information overload hurts the process of getting the "big concept" across. Many so-called idea people therefore can give a great spiel about the idea of the product, but they actually know very little about the key parameters of the things they themselves are selling.

In Xiaomi, we feel that our users are not so brilliant that they can figure out a product just from a line of advertising. We feel that the days when people bought products on the basis of ad scripting are over and won't be coming back. In our Internet communities, you can see that users scrutinize the features of a product very carefully before they buy it. They search the net for comparative products, and they get user evaluations. They even read up on how to disassemble the product. Each and every user is an expert. They understand the features of our products better than we do.

Therefore, after refining the selling points of a product, we go repeatedly through PowerPoint presentations and the product website to perfect what we want to say (Figure 3.16). I ask my salespeople to know the products and the technology behind them as well as our engineers do. Only if you are clear on everything yourself will you be able to explain it to others, and only then can you put technical jargon into a form that is comprehensible in normal language. In this process, meanwhile, you can unearth the features that are of greatest value to the users. Designers also need to know the details of product features before they can transform a product's selling points into design language.

FIGURE 3.16 *Basic source material is the lifeline of broadcasting power, or transmission.*

When we were creating the website for the Mi TV 2, a separate sound system was a new selling point. The designers and planning team put a lot of time into learning everything about the product, from decode technology to the principles behind its sound. When the product was released, we had an extremely sophisticated website to go along with it that was as complete and perfect as any international site on TV products. Users were drawn to visit the site by exquisite images on the Internet, and they then would explore product features that appealed to them from every angle. After reading our product website, they became experts on the product category, which led them to fall in love with the actual product.

A lot of product managers declare that users basically never read the fine print on websites. The interesting thing, however, is that we have had many customers call us on the customer service line after we put things out on a website to help us correct mistakes. These generally relate to punctuation marks, capitalization of technical terms, and so on—the hardest things to catch in proofreading—which means these people are indeed reading the fine print.

Every time we are getting the presentation ready for a product release, Lei Jun calls in the software engineers responsible for the technical details and asks them to sketch the principles out on a whiteboard. He says that he can know how to write the presentation only if he is clear on the underlying technology himself. Only then will he have the confidence to describe products to users. Each slide on a PowerPoint presentation, moreover, has to be designed at the level of a poster.

The marketing in Xiaomi is done through word-of-mouth reputation, and that word-of-mouth reputation is in itself a product. Therefore, the basic source material that goes into knowing the selling points for a product and how to express those selling points are the lifeline of broadcasting information about the product.

The Trick of Skillfully Deflecting When You Are Getting the Word Out

When you are creating a brand, how do you spend the least amount of money and accomplish the biggest results (Figure 3.17)?

In the early period, the main challenge was how to establish credibility. For completely new products, the quality of the product is the brand. Back then, we broke this down into several points: the star-quality level of the founding team, the reliance on the same suppliers

FIGURE 3.17 *The Trick of Skillfully Deflecting When You Are Getting the Word Out*

as Apple, the product features, and the better performance. In terms of spreading this information, we divided it into two distinct lines of attack. The official one was via the press conference when we released the product and via face-to-face interviews with media, talking about product quality. We did a lot of entertainment videos and skits as aids.

The Box Brothers

"The box brothers" were two of our employees, two chubby brothers who became extremely famous among our Mi Fans (Figure 3.18).

In a self-deprecating way, we said that it was true you could not crack walnuts with our smartphone, but our boxes were so durable that you could stand on them and they would not be squashed. The Mi 1

FIGURE 3.18 *The Images of the Box Brothers*

had a chubby person on the front page of the website. In the first set of public trials, users and the media doubted this and tried it themselves. Not only would they stand on our boxes but they would also stand on the boxes of other brands to compare them. It turned out that only our boxes stood up to the test.

The reason the box brothers became famous was that they stood on each other in a kind of pyramid on top of the Mi 2 box. In doing this stunt, our aim was to let everyone know not only about the quality of Xiaomi products but to let them know about our attitude toward doing things. Nobody could believe that we would spend RMB 10 on each and every box, when others spend RMB 2 or 3. They began to understand it when they saw that the boxes could withstand the weight of two chubby people.

Later, this image became popular source material for Photoshop among our Mi Fans. A number of variations on the theme were produced that were simply marvelous.

The funny sight of the box brothers was a kind of joke, but it also increased the trustworthiness of our brand. The Internet is essentially anti-highpoint. We therefore used an entertaining way, a kind of trick, since the most important thing was to get across an intuitive understanding. This was much more effective than having us brag about how we were one of the Fortune 500 companies.

This is related to my spoof. Many people prefer to adorn their product with a lot of highpoint adjectives. I would rather express myself in a more interesting way.

Finally, a word about what took place behind the scene as we photographed the brothers standing on that box. The photographer shot for around half an hour and took close to 100 images. At the outset, the two brothers were excited—since they mainly worked on software development backstage, they were delighted to think they would now be up there on the Internet. They thought they had better look lively. They were enraptured for the first 15 minutes, and then they began to get a little tired. Their faces sagged, particularly the one who was on the bottom. He was getting red in the face by the time the photographer finally said, okay. The photo we used was one from the end—it was more dramatic and made a bigger impact.

Each Product in Its Own Wooden Box

We defined the Mi router as a "new toy" for our fanciers. At the same time, we knew it would be the intake and out-take hub for information exchange and traffic in the Mi smart home. In the course of the open beta test (OBT), we sifted through incoming applications very carefully since we wanted to get the device into the hands of true fanciers.

We chose the option of creating a router device that could be assembled by the user. This was aligned with the spirit of geek users whom we had recruited in the beta phase, and it also enabled the user to have a direct sense of the quality of the product.

Many users take a device apart in the process of "playing" with it. We therefore went ahead and delivered it unassembled, and we had the user do it, the way IKEA ships furniture. We were fully confident in our own product, so we dared to "go naked," as it were. We allowed the user to see right down into the circuit board. It is hard to describe the sense of engagement in and the attachment to a product when you yourself have put it together. You have screwed the fan into the motherboard, put the motherboard into the case, and put the hard drive into its channel. After completing the process of assembling the router with your own hands, you really do feel you own it.

In order to provide a high-quality experience, we also added a wooden box. We made everything out of the best materials, from the outer packaging to the inside materials, from the assembly instructions to the little screwdriver. The production costs of the box alone were over RMB 200, while the total packaging came to over RMB 1,000. For this, we took only RMB 1 from the user. This playfulness was unprecedented. Even Foxconn, the highly experienced plant that did our assembly, was astonished when it learned our requirements.

This geek interest and exquisite sense startled many users, who shared assembly process on WeChat and Weibo and started competitions to assemble a router. What they were sharing with friends was not the router itself but rather their sense of accomplishment in the course of participating in the process.

After three rounds of OBT, we formally released the Mi router at the end of April 2014. In one day, we took in 3.08 million advance-purchase orders from users. At noon on the third day, the 100,000 routers that were "sold on the open market" were sold out in the space of 59 seconds.

"Each product needs its own wooden box." What we mean by this is that each has to have its own *detonation point*. First, only if a product does indeed have a detonation point can it be considered a good product, and only then does it have any chance of being successful. At the same time, a detonation point is a way of differentiating products on the basis of a sense of quality as well as functionality. It is the most effective way of displaying the uniqueness and essence of a product.

In promoting a brand, and trying to spend the least amount of money to get the biggest bang for the buck, you have to be good at using tricks. You have to be ingenious and deflect skillfully. That means having a sense of humor and using self-mockery and self-deprecation.

Holding a Dramatic PR Event

Dramatic product releases are one of the defining marks of Xiaomi. They also are the most critical link in the process of building the company's brand every year.

There is a great art to knowing how to put on a good product release (Figure 3.19). In this new type of consumer age, you need to put on events that are purely focused and that offer a great perceptual experience. Xiaomi has learned a considerable amount on its own in this regard.

First, only have a press conference if you have a "point" to make. When you release a new product, the fundamental decision-making process relates to whether or not you have a sufficiently hot event. Just having the great idea of putting on a press conference is useless if you don't have some major thing to talk about, some focal point. Just asking a hundred or so people to come hold a conference, without enough news value to generate a spark, and without enough fuel to keep that spark going, means that you never get your fire ignited.

Second, the most important "source material" in a press conference is the product itself. If you have that in hand, then all you need to do is make sure your presentation text and videos are well prepared and that you are able to explain things very clearly.

FIGURE 3.19 *Holding a Dramatic PR Event*

Nowadays, what we aim to achieve is what we call an *immersion* type of dramatic press conference:

1. To do an immersive type of press conference, the more simple and straightforward the setting, the better. The stage setup does not need to be gaudy—it is enough to have an LED screen with a black backdrop. An overly decorated scene results in too much "noise" interference.

2. The seating should be consistent—after all, everyone is there to learn about a product, not to see a fashion show. Some press conferences these days even put couches in the front row, which gives a highly inconsistent feel to the whole proceeding.

3. The length of the event should not go over 90 minutes. After that, the audience begins to feel exhausted.

4. Inside the hall, everything should be simple, and materials should be focused. Outside the hall is different—there you can have a wealth of interactive design, so that users who come early can play with products. This too relates to the form of the press conferences—we not only invite the media but more importantly we also ask our most active users to attend. We design external activities that allow them to participate, share experiences, and take home souvenirs, all of which are helpful in safeguarding a high level of excitement and anticipation about the event.

5. The very core of the press conference is the product, and the priority here is the form that presentation materials take. In preparing the key factors that will be included, you need to question yourself repeatedly and hammer home some points. How many "screaming points" will you include? Each one needs to be reasoned out in advance and organized properly. It is best to make sure that you have a screaming point every five minutes through the entire process and no restroom breaks.

In today's graphic age, a press conference is often a matter of presenting a series of images. The thing we spend the most time on therefore is preparing the script for the presentation. We aim to have poster-level images. Each should be crystal clear and easy to understand, and each should have a kind of tensile "pulling force" on the audience.

The sole star of a press conference should be the product (Figure 3.20). Only when there is sufficient material on the product can you begin to have a promotion that is amplified and passed along. Some press conferences have a pile of things unrelated to the product. For example, they ask movie stars and models to come up on stage, or they give prizes and that sort of thing, all of which are simply wrong.

Immersion means that the product has enough weight to it, its substance is sufficiently clear, and the atmosphere is concentrated enough that attendees enter completely into the transcendent state of forgetting where they are.

FIGURE 3.20 *The Press Conference*

Television Ads That Use the Ideas Behind the Internet Way of Thinking

One white good brand declared they would give up traditional advertising starting in 2014. Instead, Internet-based companies began to advertise around the Spring Festival Gala events. What happened?

Starting in around 2014, everyone in the Internet industry began talking about the Internet way of thinking about things, while people in traditional industries busily started transitioning to Internet models (Figure 3.21). The former, the Internet industry, was still putting ads in traditional media as a way to accelerate the expansion of their business and to ensure that users who were still accustomed to watching television moved more quickly to the Internet. The latter, traditional industries, now started putting less money into traditional advertising and revved up their speed to do battle on the Internet.

FIGURE 3.21 *Television Ads That Use the Ideas Behind Internet Thinking*

Xiaomi put out an ad on television in the prime time of the 2014 Spring Festival Gala. It was a one-minute branding ad that was called "Our Age."

Up to then, Xiaomi had done very little in the way of conventional marketing, yet we spent the enormous sum of RMB 60 million on this "Our Age" effort. Having amassed Internet users who then numbered in the tens of millions, we wanted to reach more of a mass market by using a conventional media platform. The prime time segment on China Central Television (CCTV), China's public television station, during the Spring Festival Gala, was our first choice. Part of our credo has always been that if we decide to do something, either we will do it well and to the ultimate excellence, or we won't do it at all. We reached total penetration.

Many branded companies have experimented with large-scale spending on brand promotion. For example, one company put much money into inviting a famous star to be a spokesperson for the company, but then they did not plan well for how to sustain the effort. The company spent RMB 5 million on the star but only RMB 10 million on the media placement. In fact, resources spent on the media should be 5 to 10 times the fees for the spokesperson. Otherwise, the strategy is invalid.

The idea behind "Our Age" was a fairly brave experiment (Figure 3.22). We only talked about the brand's qualities and feeling. Other than in the last second when the Xiaomi logo appeared, the entire ad carried no images of any Xiaomi brands or products. We were thinking solely of being the spokesperson for our Mi Fans—they were in fact the young people of "our age." Our aim was to present a kind of public service ad that declared and celebrated the emergence of this group of people.

Some people later said that our methods were rather weird, but that did not bother me at all. This ad was made for Xiaomi employees, for Mi Fans, and for our partners. As long as users liked it, as long as the people who love Xiaomi were moved by it, that was enough. Our feelings about this ad also had to do with the fact that our relationship with our users is different from other companies' relationships with their users. Normally, other brands either cheat their users by trying to brainwash them, or they pretend that the users are gods and they become obedient. We, instead, regard our users as our friends.

FIGURE 3.22 *Our Age*

This is also the reason we have never asked movie stars or other celebrities to represent us. Our products themselves are our stars, and our users are our stars. The attitude of Xiaomi itself is a kind of star. Only if users like our products, team, and our spirit will they select us, and that is precisely what we want.

One week before showing the ad for the Spring Festival Gala, we ran the premiere of the ad on the Internet, and we organized a series of events surrounding the premiere. We used all platforms to carry out the premiere, through all social media channels including mi.com, the Xiaomi BBS, Weibo, WeChat, and Qzone, as well as Baidu Tieba. We put on an activity called "Watch ad, Like, Smash golden egg, Win awards" on the Xiaomi BBS, and we encouraged fans to share the poster for "Our Age" on Weibo. We opened a topic "Our Age" on Weibo, and we put the theme music of "Our Age" in the MIUI system as a ringtone.

The activity had been going for less than 24 hours when the video had been transmitted on the Internet close to 1.5 million times. In fact, prior to the release of the ad on television, this ad had been transmitted on the Internet over 4 million times.

In adhering to the three-on-three principles of inculcating a sense of engagement, we consciously created an interactive mode for this activity that was both simple and fun. We designed a "like" activity in the Xiaomi BBS—if you liked the ad, you could hit the like button. And then you could smash a golden egg and get the opportunity to win a prize. This activity received 49 million likes. On Weibo, the topic "Our Age" was discussed in close to 200,000 messages, and more than 100,000 people downloaded its ringtone music. Countless numbers of users re-created their own special versions of the poster "Our Age" by using their own photographs.

Content is a product. The more the ideas of an ad are based on mass emotional appeal, they more the ads are suited to a participatory style of retransmission. In advance, we launched a massive "prescreening strategy" on all new media platforms. This allowed users to engage in the interactive nature of the content in advance of the actual television screening of the ad. Before the television ad was shown, we preheated on the Internet first. By the time the ad came on, we already had a base of "transmitter groups" ready to pass it on, who then served as a multiplier effect. As long as your content is good and your activities are well planned, ads too can become a kind of word-of-mouth reputation.

Many users who had seen the ad once or twice on the Internet traveled to their home base for the Spring Festival Gala and watched television with their families. As they sat there eating dumplings and then heard the sound of the distinctive music begin, they said to their family members, "Hey, come watch this. It's an ad about Mi that says nothing about smartphones. It seems interesting."

Throughout its promotion activities, Xiaomi has preserved the same feeling and quality, as reflected in the micro-movie called *Benefactors of One Hundred Dreams,* as well as the ad "Our Age." The company has "the dreams of youth," "the feeling to create a start-up," and "the positive energy." These are precisely the emotions that we want to transmit to users, partners, and the public at large. No matter how the value system of our age seems turned on its head, no matter how diversified things are becoming or what you think about "rebellious youth," humankind's desire for beauty and goodness has in fact not changed. People can use all kinds of strange methods to transmit information, and they can play all kinds of jokes in trying to get across the identity of a brand, but positive energy still trumps anything else.

I have three recommendations that sum up how to use the thinking behind the Internet to put ads on TV:

1. Use the interactivity of the entirety of networks—that is, make the TV ad be a product itself that is then put through a second round of transmission.
2. Whenever you do place ads on television, make the information as simple as possible. Make the ads focus on branding, rather than functions, as much as possible.
3. In selecting the timing and program or location of the television ad, choose the greatest platform, and concentrate your "dynamite blast"—that is, your explosive power.

For a national brand, you need to consider the combination of old media and We Media. China's population is pyramid shaped. The tip of the pyramid at the top is Beijing, Shanghai, and Guangzhou, with the population in the large cities constituting a fairly small percentage of the total. After using the Internet to "ignite" core cities, you start to cover the nationwide market, penetrating as fast as possible into second- and third-tier cities. Even if you are an Internet company, CCTV is still an extremely important option in the mix. Our strategy for putting our promotion spending into CCTV was to go for the maximum explosion, on the Spring Festival Gala, rather than investing that money in a promotion to run just any old evening.

Being the First, and Catching the Headlines

How does a tech firm make the headlines if it doesn't have any red-hot news to sell?

There is too much information in all forms of media right now. It is easy for smaller events to get drowned out by everything else, so you need to find things that are headline worthy. Only if you are first in line will you get attention.

A stunt is not enough to be a selling point for a product. An episode is also not the same as a headline.

We at Xiaomi therefore have to differentiate between stunts and selling points, headlines and episodes. That means being good at knowing what latent material can be unearthed from what you have, and then made into a headline. It means knowing what you should leave back down in the "body of the text." The tech industry has to use real products when it comes to making news. "Being the first" is the most effective strategy (Figure 3.23).

FIGURE 3.23 *Being the First and Catching the Headlines*

Social Media Marketing: The First Shot
In 2012, it was the potential headline about Weibo's trying to be commercialized. It was the initial experiment involving the entire social media network in China that Xiaomi was cooperating with Sina Weibo. In December 2012, Xiaomi and Sina jointly held an online sales event for the Mi 2 smartphone. The phones were sold solely via the Internet. The media later described this as the "first shot in social media marketing." We committed 50,000 Mi 2 smartphones to the process, and Sina was able to launch its payment function called the Weibo Wallet.

The event began at 12 noon on December 21, 2012. Within five minutes and 14 seconds, all 50,000 phones had been "snatched up" on Weibo. In addition, there had been 1.3 million users who had already made advance-order purchases. Between December 17 and 21, the account on Weibo for Xiaomi had 14.71 million hits. Other statistics were similarly impressive. There was an increase of 800,000 followers, there were 230 million exposures, and 3 million times the post was reposted about advance-purchase information. Furthermore, there were 5 million posts related to the event published on Weibo, more than 100 media companies reported on the event, and 300,000 news items were posted on Baidu. The statistics alone show that Weibo and Xiaomi had created an extremely impressive and successful marketing event.

The event was not purely a matter of combining the interests of advertising and business, however. For Xiaomi, the significance of word-of-mouth was far greater than simply the sales results. Weibo also derived tremendous returns from the event in terms of its plans to commercialize the microblog. It was this event that gave Xiaomi the confidence to go forward with cooperating with all kinds of social media platforms. It gave us a whole new understanding of the value of social media, the "base note" for writing the rest of the tune. At the same time, it set up a completely new form of win-win cooperation. The energy potential of the "explosive products" increases traffic enormously for cooperating platforms, and it enables them to show off their own value.

As a result of this initial foray, we then began a number of successful cooperative efforts with Qzone and WeChat. As a popular instant messaging service that was launched in 1999, the massive energy-potential of Qzone in particular had never been fully realized and brought to light.

Double Eleventh

The Double Eleventh is on November 11, and there is an annual flash sales event that is organized by Tmall of the Alibaba Group. When Xiaomi participated in the Double Eleventh on November 11, 2013, it came away with Four Firsts in four different categories of performance. It was first in sales volume from a single store, first in speed of reaching RMB 100 million in sales, first in sales volume in the audio-visual category, and first in focus in the brand category for cell phones. Xiaomi also ranked among the top four in sales volume for a single product.

This was already the fifth time the event had been held, and it was no longer a game solely played by Tmall, since all e-commerce players were now involved as well. Xiaomi was considered an e-commerce vendor because it had a complete e-commerce system and logistical setup, and 70 percent of its sales volume was carried by the Xiaomi network. Naturally, we wanted to be a part of this biggest e-commerce event in the country. This was our precondition to join in this game.

As with the "first shot in social media marketing" as described previously, my intent in participating in the Double Eleventh was to make headlines. In doing that, there could not be a better field of operations than this event—the results of being compared to the "big players" in the country would be quite open and obvious to all. In the most transparent way, we would be able to display our own real prowess, and we could dissolve the doubts and misunderstandings of the outside world. Prior to this event, people still had doubts about Xiaomi.

Before you get any ideas about making headlines and cooperating with others to do so, you first have to make sure your product has sufficient potential energy. Some other brands have tried to mimic Xiaomi, and they have accordingly pursued "cooperative branding." The reason the results have been modest is that their products and brands did not have sufficient potential energy. Xiaomi's star products—its Mi and Redmi smartphones—are all superior "explosive products." They are enormously liked and desired by users, which gives Xiaomi the basis for setting up cooperative online selling partnerships.

Good products speak for themselves. Only if they have that kind of power can they constantly build up brand "energy." Cooperating with outside platforms then becomes an energy amplifier. It turns potential energy into kinetic energy in the actual market, and it provides accelerating force. If the initial energy is insufficient, however, the kind of platform you use and the marketing you attempt become irrelevant. Your partners can be as willing as possible to support you, but you will still not achieve the desired results.

The Redmi is an example. Its functions, and the experience of the product, far surpassed any other products on the market at the time in the below-RMB 1,500 range of pricing. Our list price, however, was RMB 799. In the 1,000 RMB price range, it swiftly took over. The first time we cooperated with Qzone, it won us more than 10 million Mi Fans users.

"Being the first" requires a very high degree of innovation. In the space of three years, Xiaomi released three generations of the phone, and its functionality and CPU were the first out the gate, not just in terms of China but of the entire globe. The phone had the energy to make headlines.

That is why we say that the relationship between products and markets is like the relationship between 1 and 0. All of the things that come after the product, such as packaging, marketing, and promotion are for naught if you don't have the product. If the product has power, however, even if your marketing is not very good, the results will come out all right.

The Wisdom of Never Getting Angry When Dealing with Internet PR

As compared to the past, the new requirement for PR when it comes to the Internet is, "Never get angry."

Having respect for public sentiment is quite an important matter when you are dealing with the Internet. You never want to try to control this media. You also do not want to try to monopolize all outlets for public opinion when you are broadcasting your message. Public opinion nowadays is decentralized—each person can become a node for transmitting information, so it is also simply impossible to control all voices. On social media in particular, such things as misunderstandings and nit-picking are routine. As a result, what you have to do is "never get angry" (Figure 3.24). Your PR efforts on the Internet will not work if you are too thin-skinned and psychologically vulnerable.

FIGURE 3.24 *Never get angry when dealing with Internet PR.*

The Internet is a form of *attention business*. For a brand or an event to attract the attention of people on the Internet requires controversy, conflict, or some expansive force. It is not only common to have voices declare different opinions about your products but it can also be a good thing. You can benefit by taking advantage of it—the main thing is to take a firm hold of the main line and not be diverted. If 70 percent of the voices in a given situation are positive, the remaining 30 percent of negative voices are actually not that important.

For several reasons, we have to use filters to recognize these so-called negative voices, however, and to distinguish harmless misunderstandings from efforts to intentionally bring shame upon the business:

1. If negativity clearly has a business intent, is preplanned, and is threatening to become a major attack, then you have to be alert to it and deal with it when it first arises. You have to judge decidedly. As Lei Jun has always said, "We do not make trouble, but we also are not afraid of it."

2. Any products or services that are teased should receive an immediate response. Anything that can be resolved easily should receive the utmost of our efforts as soon as it happens. We should come forth with profuse apologies and promises to resolve anything soon that cannot be resolved immediately.

3. As for misunderstandings, we can generally ignore them on a policy level as long as they are not "cutting to the bone." The speed with which information moves on the Internet is so fast that misunderstandings are quickly covered over by new information.

4. For major misunderstandings that are of a significant nature, however, we need to find out the reason and resolve them through systemic revisions.

On August 16, 2011, we started releasing the Mi, and there were as many doubts about these phones are there were high expectations: Could Xiaomi actually produce and sell that many phones? How good were they?

Because of this, we began what we called Open Day events. We let people in the industry pay a visit to our first-line production facilities. There they could see for themselves each link in the process of producing, warehousing, and shipping phones. We persuaded the factories making phones for us to allow this, and we invited friends to view both the factories and our testing facilities.

By now, we have had a number of these Xiaomi Open Day activities. Many hundreds of industry people, media people, and normal users have not only made in-depth visits to our factories and seen the entire production process but they have also watched how we process orders from our official mi.com site, how our e-commerce system sends these to our circulation centers, and how products are inspected, packaged, and shipped.

This kind of transparency has, to a large degree, dispelled the inconceivable misunderstandings that people had about Xiaomi. By allowing our friends in the industry to see the entire process of product production, order taking, and order handling, we have succeeded in reducing the doubtful voices. This way of handling things has been far more effective than constantly placing ads or issuing PR statements.

There is nothing more powerful than seeing the "real thing" with your own eyes, or more moving than having people be open and frank with you.

When faced with doubts and misunderstandings, therefore, the key is to make sure that you yourself are upright and that you can respond instantly with supporting evidence. In the 2014 Mi Fans Gala, for example, we sold more than 1.3 million smartphones within 12 hours, and we received more than RMB 1.5 billion in sales. Nobody believed this, and people thought we were lying. So that evening the first thing we did was to put online the statement of payment to us from Alipay, for all to see.

Some of our branding events take advantage of humor and a sense of fun. Not only can entertainment express a certain attitude but it can also turn situations around.

The "Bet for RMB 1 Billion" happened in conjunction with the CCTV 2013 China Economic Annual Figure Awards (Figure 3.25).

FIGURE 3.25 *The Bet for RMB 1 Billion*

Lei Jun was present as the representative of the Internet "new economy," and Dong Mingzhu was present as the representative of the manufacturing "traditional economy." They were both contenders for the award. At one point, Lei Jun said that he believed the sales volume of Xiaomi could surpass that of Gree Electric's sales volume in five years, and he said, "I'll bet 1 RMB on it." The famous "iron lady" in business circles, Dong Mingzhu, head of Gree Electric, immediately pounced on this and said, "Fine, and I'll raise you to 1 billion RMB."

By our reckoning, it was likely Xiaomi would not have to wait five years to overtake Gree. The public was divided on the issue. How could we capitalize on this in the best way? Simply presenting the figures seemed uninteresting, and going around shouting slogans to show how confident we were would not do.

What we opted for was a fairly entertaining alternative. We issued a microblog message about this wager, and we invited everyone to gather around and pay attention. Sending this message out on posts meant passing along our "event microblog" at the prescribed time—no matter whether we won or lost, we would be choosing people to get an award—namely, the Mi 8. The reason we chose this model number was that we figured our new product would carry it in five years at most. As a result, this microblog had 630,000 participants who retransmitted it. In the process of this entertainment, people also came to recognize both our sense of confidence and our lighthearted attitude.

You do not have to stick rigidly to so-called proper and traditional ways to do things. As long as your facts are firmly in line with reality, you can find more powerful and incisive new ways to achieve the same ends. Relaxation and fun can get rid of unnecessary tension. In the age of media platforms, allowing the public to see you having fun may well be a better and more powerful form of PR.

CHAPTER 4

SOCIAL MEDIA

Don't Run Ads; Just Use We Media

How do you take the first step in the new marketing?

My recommendation is to let your own company become We Media: In the three-on-three principles of engagement, using We Media as both a content strategy and a brand strategy. The company must stick firmly to this approach.

Xiaomi has only two marketing channels. One is the Xiaomi network's e-commerce business. The second is its social media platforms on the Internet. The first is 70 percent of the business, and the second is 30 percent, which is precisely the opposite of many traditional firms. Instead, they rely heavily on brick-and-mortar stores. As of this writing, we have no actual physical stores at all. In 2013, Xiaomi sold a total of 18.7 million phones, which was a drop in the bucket in terms of the industry as a whole. China's smartphone market is so large that output is probably in the range of 400 million phones every year. Our sales represent less than 5 percent of that figure. Nevertheless, we are somewhat proud of the fact that we rank first, far ahead of other domestic brands, in terms of activity on platforms that have a large number of base users. That goes for Qzone, Weibo, or Youku. In March 2014, the mobile statistical report by Umeng revealed that, among the 15 most active Android system smartphones in China, only two brands were represented. One was Samsung, which had 8 of these phones, and the other was Xiaomi, which had 7 of them.

Xiaomi uses the Internet as its primary channel for sales and to maintain communications with users. What we focus on and put the priority on is not selling a certain amount of equipment. Instead, we focus on our activities with our users. The thing Xiaomi has been able to contribute as the inspiration for others in the smartphone industry is a whole new model for the smartphone business. We firmly believe that the profits from Internet smartphone sales in the future will not come from selling hardware. Instead, they will be driven by value-added business, just as is true of the Internet itself.

Faced with this self-defining attribute—committed to marketing our products via a high number of activities with our users—we needed a whole new channel to safeguard and keep up that interaction. Because of that, we have given up any traditional kind of advertising, or PR, or sales measures. Instead, we have opted for We Media—that is, social media (Figure 4.1). Furthermore, one cannot use the traditional way of thinking about "matchmakers," or intermediaries, in this new form of social media Internet business.

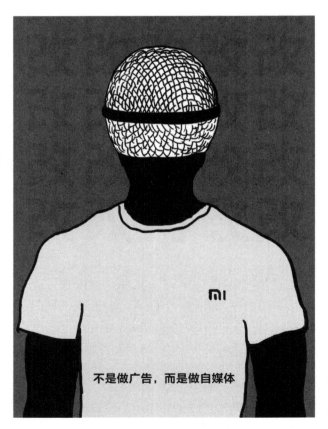

FIGURE 4.1 *Don't do ads. Just do We Media.*

The old way of thinking was that you first had to connect with the intermediary channel. Now, the first thing is to make good content. Before, you had to go in search of the right intermediary. Now, the intermediary comes looking for you. In this process, content is critical.

In terms of how to handle content when you are working with We Media, the first thing is to provide service. Marketing is secondary.

Being able to enjoy service is the force that drives users to focus on your company. "Marketing to users" is something that the company itself is concerned about—it is looking at the process from the standpoint of the company. Instead, we need to think of social media from the perspective of the user. To give an example: You like to drink Coke, but you certainly do not have to focus on Coke's microblog in order to drink it. For Coke, you need no post-transaction services, nor do you need to spend any time looking up new product information.

In our instant messaging operations, we discovered that the more products and services were integrated, the higher the rate at which users "opened" content. Things relating to new product releases had a 60 percent opening-up rate, which is five times the normal.

In developing content for We Media, we found that the most important thing was to make sure it could be understood by people easily.

I recommended what I have termed *content operations* that were in keeping with the three-on-three principles of engagement: usefulness, emotional appeal, and interactivity. *Usefulness* in this context meant not focusing on extraneous things. *Emotional appeal* meant that it could be understood by people easily, while *interactivity* meant that we could use it to guide users into enjoying the process of passing along their experience, into playing together.

In putting forth content, what we needed to express was the true experience of the product. Content did not have to be complete, but it did have to be able to find the right place on a person that would give satisfaction. Each employee involved in media operations therefore had to be someone who enjoyed playing with the product. In our company, not only do we ask that employees become fans but we also look among our fans for new employees. Many people on our operations team for social media marketing were hired from the ranks of our fans.

A counterexample to the kind of content operations I am talking about is the way traditional companies do microblog marketing. They send out highpoint messages all day, and then those messages become spam. It's hard for a user to deal with that and stay interested. If your content isn't good, then no matter how much microblog marketing you do, you'll still have poor results. You also need to avoid information overload because you don't want to be defriended by users.

Before, media was king. Now, content is king. Traditional marketing bombarded people with ads, trying to brainwash people into accepting the product concept. Instead, Xiaomi chooses face-to-face contact with its users—we ourselves are the media that we present to users.

We therefore do not create advertising. We create content.

In comparing microblog and traditional media, "follow" is the most important innovation. Behind this is the idea that the target audience changes from content to actual people. (Following is something that Twitter first put forth, and it should be considered one of the most important inventions of the Internet.)

Today, We Media in the narrow sense refers to an official account on WeChat and to a verified account on Weibo. In the broader sense, it refers to each user who has any influence.

Each individual person has become We Media, which has led to changes in the mode of transmitting information as well as receiving it. The power of the intermediary has therefore been reallocated. In the portal era, content was completely handled by the editor; in the blog era, the user participated in the editing and creation of content, but the editor still made recommendations. Now, with Weibo and WeChat, the editor is no longer in control at all.

The company has to put considerable effort into making sure it can continue to provide outstanding content, but at the same time it has to mobilize users to generate content on its behalf.

Xiaomi asks itself to carry out content operations depending on the standard requirements of each different form of social media platform. It has set up a We Media matrix, depending on the completely socialized social media platforms of Weibo, WeChat, Qzone, and Baidu Tieba. What we issue through these platforms are not Xiaomi ads but rather We Media content operations. The "academic" programs that we put on our Xiaomi BBS have mainly popularized the ways to play the smartphone, and we want to help users become experts in playing with their phones. Meanwhile, on a daily basis, users come up with new ways to use such programs as "Play Gang" and "Easy Photo," which then feed into Weibo and WeChat and are passed along.

We do not do ads. We just do We Media. Not only has Xiaomi been able to save massive amounts of money as a result but it has also set up an enormous We Media matrix that possesses tens of millions of users. As a result, we have been able to gain an unprecedented degree of close proximity to users.

The Main Battlefield: Social Media

How does Xiaomi use social media to create a national brand?

Some companies use an outsourcing company to do their social media. The idea is, "Let's just try it and see if it works." They hire some outsourcing company to help, and they take a couple of people out of their traditional operating departments and put them on this new thing. This way of doing things cannot achieve any penetration—it doesn't generate any heat. Instead, Xiaomi has invested considerable human resources in building up its social media platforms. It has more than a hundred people working on this alone, and it considers social media to be its most important marketing platform (Figure 4.2).

FIGURE 4.2 *The main battlefield is social media.*

The way in which we choose the people to do social media is also contrary to the traditional mode. Traditional companies ask marketing people to do the job. What we do is say, "We operate We Media, and what we do is content. Because of that, our social media marketing people have to be product managers, first and foremost."

We emphasize marketing that uses a product manager way of thinking. Through new media, our marketing is in direct contact with users. What's more, in contrast to the old style of marketing, the biggest difference in new media marketing is that it is no longer a one-way street. It no longer is a single-direction kind of propaganda—instead, there is information symmetry between user and company, with interaction going on at any time and in any place. Because of that, employees doing social media work must be very familiar with our products if they are to describe them clearly to users.

When I interview people for marketing positions, the emphasis is not on what channel resources or media resources they might have. Instead, I generally ask them what kind of smartphone they use, how often do they use apps and which ones, what they most like about those apps. I ask them which apps they think are best and which they would like to toss in the wastebasket. In Xiaomi, an employee's feelings about such things are what determine whether or not he or she will be good at social media marketing. Another reason for Xiaomi's success at social media marketing involves the way we internally play with each product ourselves before releasing it. Once we get the feel of it, and internalize it, we have an idea for how users will play with it, and what their attention span will be.

Xiaomi has four core channels for using social media: BBSs, microblogs, WeChat, and Qzone.

As for their attributes, microblogs and Qzone are strong, and their transmission is from one to many. They are therefore suited for doing flash events. WeChat is based on friend relationships of communications records. The transmission is one to one. It therefore is more appropriate for a customer service platform. In the early days, what we used were BBSs. Most of these were used to precipitate out established or dedicated users. BBSs are one-to-many forms of transmitting information, but they were not as fast as microblogs and could not therefore be as timely. At the same time, they resembled portals in that they still used the editor model of recommending information. It was easy for others to sift out information through automated means.

As for user relations, the weaker your relationship with users, the less the sense of trustworthiness they will transmit on your behalf, and the weaker will be the results of participatory word-of-mouth reputation. WeChat provides the strongest relationship. The next are Qzone and BBSs, while the last are microblogs (Figure 4.3). This applies particularly to a lot of verified accounts on microblogs—99 percent of these users are of the weak relationship type.

FIGURE 4.3 *Microblogging websites are the number one social media websites.*

In using social media to set up a word-of-mouth reputation, Xiaomi ensures that the features of its products are integrated into the process. Our core users are fans, and they are our end users. When they first started using our products, such as using the MIUI to install new firmware on their smartphone, the barrier to entry was extremely high. Information would be too fragmented if we relied solely on microblogs for transmission, and it would then be hard to sift through and precipitate out users. That is why we then constructed our BBS. Once we had precipitated out several hundred thousand core users by using the BBS, we could then start to use the microblogs and Qzone methods of promoting a word-of-mouth reputation about our products.

I should note that other companies face all different kinds of situations. Because of that, when they are constructing their own social media channels, the core issue is to look at the requirements of the product itself. For example, take Huangtaiji's pancakes—that company does a pretty good job of promoting itself on microblogs, and they in fact don't need BBSs to get users to go deeply into product features. After all, users don't need to discuss whether a griddle cake tastes better with 100 sesame seeds on it, or 101!

By June 2014, Xiaomi had 20 million users on BBSs, 30 million on Qzone, and over 6 million each on Weibo and WeChat. We have an enormous amount of traffic on our BBSs—every day, we get over 2 million visitors, and the daily "invite to participate" is over 300,000, which is 10 times that of similar firms.

How do we measure our brand influence these days? We mainly look at index.baidu.com and top.taobao.com. The first of these is a market index; the second is a sales index.

In June 2014, Xiaomi was always in the top three on index.baidu.com for the smartphone product and brand category. Behind this was the fact that we have considered word-of-mouth reputation about good products to be of primary importance, and we have remained firmly with social media as the main battlefield for our marketing efforts.

Microblogs: The Most Popular Type of Social Media

How do we use microblogs to stir up excitement among users and generate a sense of engagement? We generate topics through both events and through our content itself.

When we first started operations on microblogs, we summed up three main lessons:

1. Use the microblog account or user name as you would a website, in terms of operating approach.
2. Use microblog topics as the channel on a website.
3. Absolutely do not put overuse messages on microblogs.

We recruited many capable people. We created an entire team for handling microblog operations, including a product manager, an editor and assistant editor, a designer, and a software engineer. The second item came about as the result of feeling our way forward in operations and summing up a set of lessons. We then assigned a person specifically to each long-term topic and handling its needs, and we constantly updated the features of each topic.

An example would be our topic relating to "Anytime Photo." This encouraged people to share photos of key moments with others via our microblogs. The effectiveness of this topic was most apparent at around noon every day because that was when young people would get together for a meal and take photos of one another; plus the light was good, and it was easier to photograph.

The topic "Play Gang" introduced all kinds of new and unusual ways to use and play with electronic products. The effectiveness of this was most apparent in the morning, probably because people tended to get to work and check out any new and interesting content on the Internet. Topics relating to Mi-terms, such as the one about chicken soup for the soul, were most effective when they were put out at night.

The item relating to "Don't overuse messages on the microblogs" was the hardest for many companies on Weibo to grasp hold of. From the outset, Xiaomi drew a "red line" for itself. Other than major activities, such as a press release, daily messages put on the microblogs were not to exceed 10 lines.

Here are three case studies of how Xiaomi has used Weibo in its operations.

Case 1. "I Am a Phone Fancier"
In addition to content, we use events to strengthen the sense of users' engagement. The very first activity we did on Weibo was called "I am a phone fancier" (Figure 4.4). We did not put a single penny into promotion, but within a very short time, this activity generated 1 million user-participants. Users showed off their phones and how they had used them so far, and they described their experiences with their phones.

FIGURE 4.4 *"I am a phone fancier."*

The most apparent demonstration of group consciousness on the Internet relates to the desire to display yourself, to "shine," and thereby get a heightened sense of the feeling that you yourself count. This phenomenon began to appear in the period when the digital age began intermingling with and transitioning out of the late Industrial Age. People can see much the same rationale behind all interactive activities on the Internet. For example, the apps called Baidu Motu asked users to figure out which movie star they felt was most similar to photos of themselves. They then had users superimpose their own face over the face of the movie star. The sense of engagement in this process was intense—it satisfied the users' own desires to shine and gave them the sense that they too existed. As a result, it was highly successful. Another success should be noted here—a very famous game called Bomb Plane on WeChat. Thanks to users' desire to show off, and their desire to win, many friend groups competed against one another to the point that their fingers got numb. The minute you had good results, you could share your triumph with all.

"I am a phone fancier" had a certain backstory to it. In July 2011, we had just announced that we were going to make smartphones. Although Xiaomi had 500,000 users of MIUI at the time, the whole smartphone market was pretty much unknown territory to the company. The question became how to get users who had never seen a Mi become familiar with Xiaomi as a brand at first.

We came up with the idea of an activity that had users bask in the glory of demonstrating how they had used their own phones. As phone fanciers, what did we ourselves like most? We liked showing off before friends in demonstrating the various games we had played on our phones. Since Xiaomi was "born for fans," we decided, Why not have an activity that allowed fans to show off?

At that time, Weibo could only transmit text and images. If we had operated in the traditional way, that would probably have just involved asking users to select their own text and images and put them up for viewing. This involved quite a high barrier to entry, however, since users would have to spend a lot of time on it, thinking over the text and photos they wanted to use. Plus it was hard to organize photos on the phones many people had used in the past. People had also forgotten the model names they once used, and so on.

The enthusiasm with which users get involved is a key to success, so ideally you provide them with the most convenient tools. What we did, therefore, was to create a product called "I am a phone fancier." This provided tools right there on the page. All the users had to do was select the models they had used in the past from a list. Their selection would then automatically create a Weibo graphic and line of text. Once the users pushed the button, they could share their phone history with all those they communicated with on Weibo.

Not only was this kind of tool convenient for users but it also reduced the rate at which users lost enthusiasm for something due to the nuisance of having too much to handle. It preserved a high rate of effective retransmission. It also enabled the page that was shared to be visually effective since it was well designed. The potential energy that was transmitted along with the page was therefore much more powerful.

In order to increase users' ability to show off their prowess and shine, we also helped them figure out how much they had spent on their phones automatically. Users could choose to write a small passage about each phone they had used—we originally thought they actually would not opt to do this and that they would skip over this item, but we discovered that many users actually wrote very detailed and marvelous descriptions of each phone they had owned.

This experience was of ultimate importance. It was a critical step in going from broadcasting purely information as content to making the broadcast itself become a product. At the same time, it set us firmly on the path of deciding to use dissemination via social media as our main battlefield. These two points became the core characteristics of what later came to be called "Xiaomi style communication."

On the evening that this product went online, it was retransmitted more than 100,000 times almost instantly, which far surpassed our anticipation. One has to remember that the influence at the time was almost nil. What's more, this activity did not simply involve hitting a button. It required the users to go one by one through the options on our event page and check off the phones that they had used in the past. If the users did not do the whole thing, which took several minutes, they could not complete the activity and participate.

It was already quite late in the evening by the time the product went online, and the R&D team who had been managing it were exhausted. They had worked on this launch for days. They were all getting ready to go home to rest, when they saw the explosive way the thing had taken hold. They immediately decided to keep up the pace by continuing to make changes and continuing the interactive process. Later they again changed the interface so as to improve the smooth functioning of the activity.

As we continued to make improvements, we put this activity into the scope of responsibilities of the Xiaomi BBS. When each new user signed into a Xiaomi BBS, he or she would be guided to list the phones that he or she had used in the past. We later made a function that made this easy, and the history of the phones users had used in the past could then be shared over Weibo. As a result, even though we officially worked on this for no more than a few days, and even though we did no further upkeep on the activity page, users kept using it. To this day, users sometimes come into this activity page and conscientiously fill out their total history with phones. That is then shared with their user groups on Weibo.

Behind the success of this case study was the kind of thinking that uses products themselves to generate transmission. Without famous people reposting, fancy copywriting, and the incentive of getting prizes, we simply put out Internet "products" that people themselves liked. These products were fun. They pulled people in and engaged them, whether that was out of nostalgia for their former days or whether it was out of wanting to shine in front of others.

Up to now, "I am a phone fancier" has been discussed as a topic on Weibo over 1.7 million times. As of March 2014, there were still several hundred users participating in broadcasting their information on this every single week. It should be noted that Xiaomi did not spend a single penny on advertising in order to generate this kind of activity.

Case 2. Our 150 Grams Youth

Could we possibly do a product release solely online?

In May 2012, when we were getting ready to launch the youth version of the Mi, we decided to try a fairly courageous experiment: releasing the product without any offline press conference at all and just doing the initial release on Weibo (Figure 4.5).

FIGURE 4.5 *The Packaging of the Youth Version of the Mi*

One and one-half months prior to the release, we did some warm-up activities on Weibo by putting out a film on the topic of "Our 150 Grams Youth." This portrayed classic scenes of people's college days. It did not actually say what kind of product was going to be issued, however, and the anticipation continued all the way up to the initial release on Weibo.

FIGURE 4.6 *Our 150 Grams Youth*

The classic scenes used the seven of us partners as material. We took off for an afternoon and went to the dormitory of the Central Academy of the Arts, which was close to our office. There, we shot a short film that we called *Our 150 Grams Youth*. In this film, you can watch each of us doing bizarre things: Lei Jun is trying to direct the film, I am fiddling with a camera, KK is waiting for his date, Hong Feng is hanging up some smelly socks, while Lin Bin is sitting there reading *The Forbidden Legend Sex & Chopsticks*. Liu De is playing a guitar, and Dr. Zhou is playing electric aircraft. As soon as this film came out, we had users wanting to buy a copy of Lin Bin's *The Forbidden Legend Sex & Chopsticks*, as well as one of the T-shirts printed with "adiaos" (*adiaos* means a nobody) that KK was wearing. In fact, The *Forbidden Legend Sex & Chopsticks* that he was reading was simply an empty notebook with blank pages. Given the clamor for this anyway, as well as the T-shirt, we immediately printed up 5,000 empty notebooks and had 10,000 T-shirts produced, and all of these sold out within an afternoon. To this day, these two remain some of our bestselling products.

The youth version of the phone was aimed at students as the core users. The packaging was particularly elegant and scholarly, and it looked like a book cover, the name on which was *Xiaomi Youth*. In planning to roll this out on Weibo, we thought up a sentence to go with it: "The soul of humanity weighs 21 grams, but our youth version of the phone is 150 grams."

After that, we quietly paid our respects to the film *You Are the Apple of My Eye*, and we added an online poster to the initial release. We shared the poster on Weibo with two messages (Figure 4.7). One message was reposted 2 million times and received 1 million comments, and the second message was reposted more than 1 million times. This record number of interactions was not surpassed until the end of 2012, when we ourselves broke the record with a different Weibo activity. The press conference that we held on Weibo for this product enabled us to sell 150,000 phones right away, and the results of the activity went far beyond what anyone had imagined.

How was the activity successful? First, it surpassed our sales target for the product ahead of time. Second, it set the record at the time for the number of participatory reposts on Weibo. Everyone assumed we had

FIGURE 4.7 *The Poster of the Youth Version of the Mi on Weibo*

used Weibo for the broadcast in order to have some kind of drawing for a prize. Later, however, a number of companies who were selling products that were far more expensive than Xiaomi did try such a drawing, but the repost results were an entire grade lower than ours had been in terms of quantity. As I see it, the core reason was that these other companies did not understand how to generate a sense of user engagement. They looked on the interactive segment of the process as the end goal, so they ultimately came up short. A purely material incentive is effective only for a short time, and it is often only supported by a bunch of "deadbeats" who are professionals at getting prizes.

To us, the most important thing was that this activity flowed into and became a part of Xiaomi's own corporate mystique.

After that, "youth" became a key term in Xiaomi's language. We no longer call that model a "youth" phone, but the terms "youth," "hot-blooded feelings," and "dreams" all became part of the Xiaomi product culture. This extended to the films that we made later, including *Benefactors of One Hundred Dreams* and *Our Age*.

Case 3. Borrowing the Force from Others, as in the Case of the Teleplay
My Love from the Star

"Borrowing a ride from others" is a knack that social media people must learn to do. The question here was how to make use of Weibo content in the cleverest way.

In early 2014, a teleplay named *My Love from the Star* and made in South Korea was being shown throughout Asia, and it had already been a hot broadcast for more than two months. The female lead in this drama at one point said, "On the night of the first snow, one really should drink beer and eat fried chicken." Because of the popularity of this teleplay, the words became a kind of catchphrase among all the fans.

By February 27, the grand finale of the teleplay was approaching. That noon, Xiaomi issued a photograph on Weibo. The photo was of a notice in the Xiaomi cafeteria (Figure 4.8): "The final episode of *My Love from the Star* is showing late tonight. If Qian Songyi [the heroine in drama] is not back together with Du Minjuan [the hero in drama] by that time, Xiaomi will be providing free beer and fried chicken on Friday as a consolation. We ask all departments to organize this in advance, so that everyone can get his or her share in orderly fashion."

This blog post had such a human touch to it, and it was also so in tune with the topic of the day, that it was quickly transmitted thousands upon thousands of times.

At noon on the second day, the official account of Xiaomi on Weibo followed this with a news item: "Whether it snows today or not, and no matter how the ending turns out, we welcome my love from the star for free beer and fried chicken. To celebrate, we are dropping the price of the 2S model to RMB 400! PS: The boss says that fellow students who drink too much do not have to show up in class next morning. Those who see this are the lucky ones—everyone who wants to come, please raise your hand!" At the same time, mi.com uploaded a series of protective covers for phones that were designed specifically with "fried chicken and beer" in mind. As can be expected, these accessories were instantly snatched up by the teleplay's fans.

Weibo must master the art of riding the wave, which means taking advantage of the prevailing situation in how they conduct their sales. The examples given above of being "I am a phone fancier" and *Our*

通知

鉴于《来自星星的你》今晚凌晨播放大结局，如果千颂依没有和都敏俊在一起，周五午餐食堂将提供免费啤酒和炸鸡，以示安慰。届时，请各部门安排好就餐时间，有序领取。

小米公司餐饮部
2014. 2. 27

FIGURE 4.8 *The Notice in the Xiaomi Cafeteria*

150 Grams Youth, and of "fried chicken and beer," are ways in which we did this. There are many other superlative examples of how other companies have done this on Weibo as well. One would be the classic blog statement of Durex, which is an absolute textbook example: "Thin is going to have an accident sooner or later." ("Thin" has the same pronunciation with the Chinese word "bo." When Chinese official Bo Xilai was under investigation, Durex sent out this statement on Weibo.)

Qzone and Its Younger Generation

Qzone is often overlooked as a social media platform on which to carry out broadcasting and to amplify your message. However, it is the primary stomping grounds of the younger generation.

The user group of Qzone is mainly composed of people below the age of 25 (Figure 4.9). Analysis of the data shows that Qzone users particularly like to transmit photos via this medium, and more than 70 percent of the photos are taken with a smartphone. Among photos that are transmitted using the Android system, Mi ranks number one.

FIGURE 4.9 *Qzone and Its Younger Generation*

There are two lessons to be learned from Qzone operations:

1. There are similarities between Qzone and Weibo products in that they both have the attribute of being a medium that transmits and reposts information on the Internet, which makes them both appropriate for flash sales or event marketing. However, their users have different demographic profiles. Qzone users are younger than those on Weibo.

Weibo users generally consider themselves to be opinion leaders, and they like to express their own point of view. In contrast, Qzone users are happy to like posts and to simply say that they know about it or that they think it is "okay."

2. Qzone has a higher click-through rate (CRT) than Weibo for external links in the content. This means that the high rate of "linkage hits" can cause users to enter into mi.com, which brings us quite substantial traffic. This is extremely important for an enterprise that is engaged in e-commerce.

The Initial Release of Redmi, Conducted Completely Online

The Redmi is positioned to suit a younger audience. It has a "screamingly" low price, and it has top-rate hardware in that price category. In order to target its user group precisely, we decided to use Qzone for the initial release of the product.

On the afternoon of July 29, 2013, an illustration suddenly appeared on the Internet that said, "Xiaomi is going to be releasing a mystery product priced within RMB 1,000, which will be released exclusively on Qzone." This stirred up interest and curiosity about what the product might be, and some media sources were even reporting that it might mean that Tencent was buying shares in Xiaomi.

At the time, Qzone had already been operating for quite a while in China, and it had an immense user base. Its market share of application types of products on China's Internet was far in advance of anyone else—it reached some 130 million people in terms of coverage. Nevertheless, it was not very sure about how to use this asset or how to explore new businesses and unearth new business models that took advantage of social networking sites (SNSs). It also lacked a good "detonation point," so that it had not received the recognition it deserved within the industry.

Prior to this time, Xiaomi had operated in the social media sphere by using only the Xiaomi BBS and Weibo. It had no precedent for using any other platform to carry out sales activities. Qzone seemed perfect for our needs, however, since its young users were particularly price sensitive as well as attuned to functionality. This was precisely the target audience for the Redmi. Xiaomi and Qzone therefore quickly struck up a deal.

In July 2013, phones like the Redmi with an MTK quad-core processer CPU and a 4.7-inch touch screen generally sold at a list price of around RMB 1,500. At the time, everyone was guessing that the price of the Redmi would be between RMB 999 and 1,299. Among mainstream phones, its hardware was outstanding, and it operated on a smooth MIUI system. Since it was in fact priced at RMB 799, it completely detonated the market by going through Qzone to become a "phenomenon" product.

Xiaomi cooperated with Qzone, which involved an advance ordering event to stir up attention. We did a price-guessing activity in which more than 1 million users participated within the first 30 minutes. Once advance ordering began, more than 5 million users participated in advance ordering within the first three days. By August 12, on the day before Xiaomi actually began to sell, more than 7.45 million Qzone users had ordered the phone in advance.

On the actual day of selling, we had nobody lining up at stores in the usual fashion with an absolute sea of people trying to get the phone. All activity was online. Nevertheless, we did have a massive force of online activity: within the first second, 148,000 users had hit the buy button, and within the first minute and a half, 100,000 Redmi had been completely sold out.

Prior to selling the Redmi on Qzone, Xiaomi had 1 million fans on this social media site. By August 12, after the Redmi sale, Xiaomi's fans on Qzone numbered 10 million.

We cooperated again with Qzone in March 2014, to release the product called the Redmi Note. More than 1.5 million users made advance purchases, and fans on Qzone went to 30 million.

New Ways of WeChat

We operate differently on WeChat than we do on other forms of social media.

If you try to use WeChat as a sales platform, you will be going up a dead-end alley. WeChat is more appropriate to being a service platform, given the way it records friend relationships in its communications (Figure 4.10).

WeChat was just getting popular in June 2012, so I began talking to my colleagues about the possibility of using WeChat as a We Media form. At that time, people inside the company were somewhat hesitant. I asked the people in charge of the Xiaomi network to stop using MiTalk temporarily and instead use WeChat for three months. They did this from September to December, to get an idea of how to use WeChat as We Media in our operations.

By February 2013, we had decided to use WeChat, and we then started forming a team in earnest to work on it. Within less than one year, the number of our fans in the official account on WeChat exceeded 5 million, which was one of the largest official accounts.

We set up three navigation tags in the official account: New Activities, Self-Help Services, and Products. By hitting any of these tags, you would

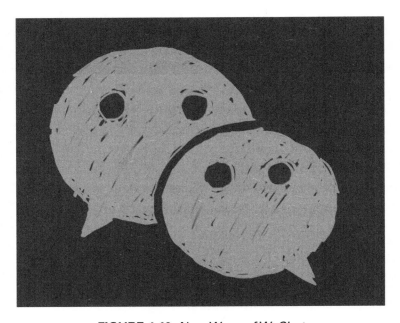

FIGURE 4.10 *New Ways of WeChat*

get a response automatically. For Self-Help Services, you could then search your order, the location of the local Mi Home, and so on. For Products, you could look up any question you might have about Xiaomi products and get an answer.

When the number of fans on WeChat went to 800,000, the back-office information volume became too great to handle one by one. Through an application programming interface (API) connection of the official account, we developed a special customer service back-office platform. This connection had a number of customer service user accounts that ensured that many customers could be online at the same time. User questions could be responded to simultaneously by customer service, but in addition, this displayed who successfully had resolved issues, how the issues had been resolved, and to what extent they had been resolved. All of this was shared information that could be viewed by everyone. In addition, we set up key terms that were handled automatically. For example, if you keyed in "Mi 3," the back office would resolve your issues through automatic responses. We did as much as possible to have customer servicing done through self-servicing methods by smart-information responses. In 2013, the number of fans who contacted us through WeChat exceeded 50 million hits, of which 10 percent were handled through automated responses.

Our back office also had an automated *prize-drawing function*. When we were doing activities on WeChat, this prize-drawing activity would go through the back office programming (to do the drawing), which ensured that it was all done fairly and properly. We even took videos of the prize drawings and put them up on the Xiaomi BBS, which increased the confidence of users and made them more inclined to continue participating in the prize activities.

People may wonder how in fact we increased the number of fans on WeChat. Of the total group of our WeChat fans, 60 percent belonged to the official account, 30 percent were extended by activities on WeChat, and another 10 percent were from external forms of cooperation. In other words, because there were so many ways people became fans, the fan activity on WeChat has been extremely high.

In May 2013, when the number of fans on WeChat was just 600,000, we tried out the idea of adding a Friend Code, that is, an F Code, to our interactions on WeChat. Within just one day, 450,000 F Codes had been issued, and the number of fans had increased by 250,000. After we got an F Code, our sales volume reached RMB 55 million.

In July 2013, once our experience with the Redmi promotion via Qzone was recognized as highly successful, we decided to do another new-product release on WeChat. We had the opportunity in late 2013 when WeChat uploaded a payment function as a way to increase its bank card volume. We cooperated with Tencent in doing a special session for Mi 3 promotion on WeChat. As a result, within 9 minutes and 55 seconds, we had sold 150,000 Mi 3 phones, and at the same time we increased the number of our fans by 1.8 million, to a total number of 4.4 million fans.

Our experience has been that we can pull in a large number of new fans via the official account on WeChat by planning large-scale events. However, the effectiveness of this method diminishes if we repeat the same old forms of events. Because of this, it is not enough to use the prize-drawing incentive on our official account. Operations personnel have to make constant innovations and design new forms of fun activities. We also need to put adequate funding into this effort if we want to increase the fan base quickly.

I frequently say to people in the company: when the platform changes, the way of the operation has to change as well.

In using social media, you have to make sure you accommodate the qualities of each different type of social media. For example, for Weibo, you have to use interesting content and appropriate prize incentives. You need to give users a reason to forward your message. For Qzone, you need to get users to like your posts by your posting the right content. For ZhiHu, which is a question-and-answer platform, you need technical information. WeChat is inseparable from smartphones. For example, one of the key functions of WeChat is the sound of a voice.

We therefore decided to try something fun with this voice function of WeChat. In December 2013, we designed an activity called "Shout out" on WeChat. This was not an effort to get people to repost messages as a way of getting a chance to win a prize. It was simply shouting. The only action users had to take was to shout the words, "I love Mi!" and then send the voice message to our official account. We then ranked the user messages according to the decibel level of the voice. High-decibel users had the chance to win a prize, but they also had the right to buy a Mitu at an extremely preferential price.

This kind of interaction between users and the company seemed quite new and fresh, and once it went online, we soon received over 300,000 users' voice messages. Naturally, some users shouted more than once. In order to get a higher ranking, some users went crazy screaming into their phones, to the extent that it brought on problems with neighbors.

At the end of this activity, 10,000 Mitu were purchased in the space of a few minutes.

Xiaomi BBSs: Home of Our Older Customers

How do you use traditional BBSs to precipitate out fans?

We often talk about "updating Weibo" or "hitting BBSs," but these are two different activities. On Weibo, for example, let's say you have a very appealing topic that pulls in "eyeballs" and that attracts people to focus on you and talk about you, which even gives them a "sense of existence." Tomorrow you don't have that topic, however, and people go elsewhere to surround someone else. On BBSs, however, at a certain point people get used to coming to you. Like hitting the bar, they may just come look things over when they don't have anything better to do, or they want to chat with people they've met there. They want you to know what their opinions are on this and that. In this way, the BBSs allow you to "sift out" or "precipitate" users (Figure 4.11).

One finds further differences between the two by going a step further:

1. **Form of content.** Content on Weibo is fragmented. But on the BBSs, content can be focused on special topics—the medium is more suited to going deeply into subjects for ongoing transmission. For example, you can use BBSs to introduce ways to install firmware or to take photographs more effectively.

FIGURE 4.11 *Xiaomi BBSs are the home of our older customers.*

2. **Structure of the user group.** Weibo basically has a horizontal structure of users because users have so few options for responding to content: like or dislike, confirm or reject. On BBSs, the user relationship is more pyramidal in shape (Figure 4.12). It is more like an organization or an association, and it is driven more by quantitative accomplishment so it is more professional.

Put more colloquially, Weibo is like a public square, whereas is BBS is more like a club. The orientation of Xiaomi in the way it uses its BBSs is not only to make them like a club but also to make them like a home.

Once products are sold, they in fact also become content, in that images, videos, and text that are generated by that product constitute the resulting content. In the past, traditional firms simply made their own content. They would hire people or media to create endless messages about their products. Nowadays, by way of contrast, users themselves create messages on BBSs that put out vast amounts of content about your products. For example, we have a public-trial platform called the

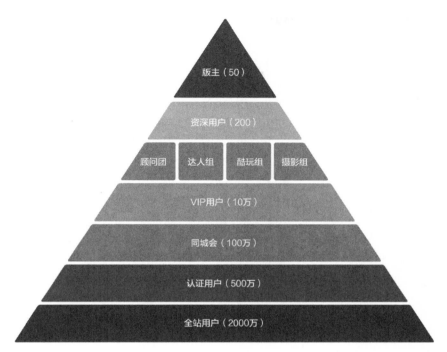

FIGURE 4.12 *The Structure of the User Group on the Xiaomi BBS*

"Xiaomi Play Gang," which has several hundred ways to test and evaluate premier products under the Product Purchase tag. And those hundreds of ways are just for premier products.

The BBS is one of the most ancient services on the Internet. Meanwhile, China's earliest portal on the Internet was Sina, which was born out of a BBS. When the Xiaomi BBS was just getting started, it was primitive. It began on August 16, 2010, with just one engineer in the back office, who put simple codes online as a BBS. In the first month, there were only a hundred or so registered users. At that time, Xiaomi had only a few dozen employees, most of whom were either software engineers or designers. It had nobody at all who knew how to operate a BBS. We found an engineer to do it, who tried it out in addition to his regular job.

Nowadays, programming code that is developed for a BBS is highly sophisticated in terms of both functions and ways to operate with it—you could even say this is overdone. There are user ranks, user points, virtual money, medals, tasks, voting, prize drawings, and so on. The Xiaomi BBS over the past four years has basically stayed within the scope of these things from a purely functional standpoint. However, in the span of these four years, the Xiaomi BBSs have amassed gained 20 million registered users and 200 million posts in total. Meanwhile, the BBSs are constantly changing and undergoing a process of trial and error, just as the MIUI is generated every week. New innovations and improvements range from the domain name to layout, from the channels to the content.

When you have 20 million users, the critical issue becomes how to construct the *user relationship*. What we have decided is that it should be pyramidal in shape, with users mainly helping and managing other users while the official team stays in the background, helping the core user team handle the BBS itself.

Below are several case studies that illustrate how we operate our BBSs.

Case 1. The F Code That Provides Old-Time Users with Special Privileges
The F Code is what we call a *micro-innovation* that provides Xiaomi members with special rights. It was not generated from any desire to do marketing but rather from a desire to have older users get the first chance to experience our new products.

In 2011, after we released the Mi, the "explosion" was far beyond what we had anticipated would happen. This presented our operating credo with some problems with respect to our relationship with Mi Fans. A lot of older users, who were by now deeply participating in the process of improving MIUI, were in fact unable to buy one of our phones. To address this, we invented the F Code, which stands for Friend Code. We designed a special system whereby certain users could be first in line to purchase products on our e-commerce platform by using a code.

Later, a number of other companies copied the practice and put out this or that "code." These looked similar to the F Code, but they produced far less results. The reason is that they were looking at the F Code in a superficial way, without understanding the true reason it came into being. Without the friends relationships that are behind an F Code, you can't begin to create the kind of intimate relationship that only good friends develop.

As Xiaomi grew and developed, users are what provided us with our most important support. Whenever a new Mi first came on the market, it was hard to obtain—we therefore provided the F Code to enable these key users to be first in line to experience our newest products. The fundamental reason behind designing the F Code was to allow users to experience the real thing—to do that, we definitely were happy to provide them with special privileges.

Case 2. "Courageous Intelligence Storms the Pass" That Motivated Users' Desire to Win

In operating the BBS, quantitative results are more important than material incentives.

The Mi 3 was released on September 5, 2013. The question then became how best to enable users to appreciate its superior capabilities.

"Courageous Intelligence Storms the Pass" was an activity that we designed specifically with this in mind. It was created to enable our users to take the initiative themselves in gaining product understanding through their interactions on the Xiaomi BBS.

FIGURE 4.13 *"Courageous Intelligence Storms the Pass"*

The principles behind the activity were quite simple. This was a question-and-answer exercise. We would provide users with 10 choices for topics as prepared within our topic bank. The user could then answer the questions within the topic and get points. The questions were all related to the Mi 3. For example, what kind of lens did it have, how large was it, how far could the Bluetooth 4.0 transmit a signal, and so on.

A lot of people could simultaneously engage in this question-and-answer activity, but how could Xiaomi make sure that enough users did indeed participate? How could Xiaomi make sure that when users played with the online activity, they were not merely coming to win a prize but would have that deeper sense of participating in something?

In addition to encouraging users to share on Weibo, Qzone, and so on, which was necessary, we also designed the activity "Courageous Intelligence Storms the Pass" to be a task on the Xiaomi BBS. As soon as a user logged in on the BBS, the system would remind the user that he or she had not yet done the new task for the day. This task did not take the position of an ad, but it was more effective than an ad in promoting the activity.

Traditionally, the design of an activity emphasized doing things that were as simple as possible so as to let the users participate easily. If it were the question-and-answer type of activity, the correct answers had to be fairly obvious. This was to let the users feel good about getting them right. That logic was all right as far as it went. Nevertheless, we wondered if we could go against this logic and see if the opposite worked as well.

In the activity "Courageous Intelligence Storms the Pass," we designed questions that were not as easy or obvious. If the users were not very familiar with the Mi 3, for instance, it would be hard to simply guess the correct answer. The result was that users actually loved this. Once we released the activity, many fans would do it over and over again, after realizing they initially had gotten only 60 points, or 50, or even just 40. Instead of discouraging our older users, this kind of setback encouraged them to try harder the next time. It was like playing a game. We had prepared a topic database with several hundred topics, so that whenever users entered the question-and-answer session, they would always be confronted with new questions. Whenever they couldn't answer, they would conscientiously go to the Novice Entry program and look things up.

The result of this activity was that hard questions did not in fact affect the feeling of engagement in the game but, on the contrary, made users participate even more vigorously. By the time this activity was basically over, it had been played more than 21 million times by more than 2 million users. On average, each person had answered questions more than 10 times.

Case 3. A Directly Transmitted Product Release That Generated a Sense of Engagement

Prior to Xiaomi, the great majority of product releases in China were put on just for the media. For us, however, product releases were not purely for the media but also for our users, for Mi Fans. On August 16, 2011, Xiaomi held a product release, and more than half of the 600 participants were users. Later, this was the case as well, when we put on product releases for over 2,000 people.

Even with 2,000 people, however, this number was miniscule when it came to letting users understand the products from the very first minute. It became necessary to try to use our official platform as a way to transmit directly our product releases.

When the press releases product information, the things they think about are the news points that they can include. In slightly different fashion, what users focus on are the selling points the new product might have. They focus on such things as what Xiaomi has actually produced, when it will be available, what other users are saying about the product, are there any activities that might give them preferential treatment, and do they have any friends who were going to be at the product release.

As a result, when we directly transmitted a product release on our BBSs, we carefully considered each and every detail that would be included. At the very beginning, this involved simply text. Later, it incorporated images, and finally also videos. In addition to the activities on the day of the actual release, moreover, which went from 2 p.m. to 4 p.m., we also spent the prior week introducing related content on our BBSs. We broadcast the progress we were making in preparations for the release, and we alerted people that other famous fans were planning to attend. Once they arrived in Beijing, we reported on their every move. We put together graphics and text almost like a tourist agency. We explained where people coming in from outside Beijing could go to eat and enjoy themselves. If they were coming from the airport, we explained how to get to the hall. If they were coming from the train station, we explained which exit to take, how to catch public transportation, where they could get on, where they could get off, which exit of the subway to use, then whether they should turn right or left once they emerged, and so on.

In 2011 and 2012, we simply used the traditional form of text and images during the product releases. By September 2013, up to seven or eight days before the next event, we kept on asking ourselves if we couldn't do something a little different. What could we do to increase the users' sense of engagement?

As a result, we again made ourselves crazy. At the last minute we decided to do something outrageous. Some colleagues and I from the Xiaomi BBS brainstormed on this until the early morning hours. The basic form of the BBS posting was an invitation. The question was, how could we improve upon this invitation, to make it more innovative? Finally, we decided we would let the users not just look at the thing but also play with it. Not only could they play with it, moreover, but they could also play with users on other BBSs. Although there was just one week left before the product release, we called together a group of software developers and developed two brand-new interactive functions. These were called "breaking the golden egg," and "sending gifts." As users participated on the BBSs and as they watched the progress of the product release, they could concurrently play the golden egg game. As they played the game, they could send digital gifts to their friends.

As the entire press conference was going on, we issued more than a hundred different types of invitations on the Xiaomi BBS. Later, in the form of a general invitation to the product release, we assembled all of these into a general report. The direct transmission of the product release continued online for a week, and several million people participated by visiting the site. On September 5, 2013, at the annual meeting of Xiaomi, the general invitation that was put on the Xiaomi BBS had more than 1.3 million users simultaneously participating, while more than 1 million users responded to the invitation.

More than a million: that is the power of users' having a sense of engagement!

CHAPTER 5

SERVICE

People Are More Important Than Systems

How can you use the "thinking that underlies the Internet" for customer service?

The traditional form of customer service puts a focus on systems and KPIs. With respect to customer service in Xiaomi, however, my own feeling is that people are more important than systems (Figure 5.1).

FIGURE 5.1 *People are more important than systems.*

The people in charge of our customer service had just come into the company when I met with them for a long time, exchanging views on how this work should be done. They had done extremely well in their previous jobs in large companies, and they been in charge of major flowchart types of procedures, with a lot of methodology behind them. In traditional customer service, KPIs are important, such as rate of input, rate of throughput, and how many cases are received in 30 seconds, including the figures for each individual. I told them that they had to forget about all these things. They had to forget all they had done before. Those things endorsed them professionally, but our concepts were quite different.

Customer service does not focus on KPIs in Xiaomi. Target figures are used as a reference, but what really counts is "making friends with users." The idea is that having people providing good service from their own sense of accomplishment is much more important.

The head of our customer service department had been in the business of customer service for over a dozen years, and she had considerable experience. In 2012, the business took off, and the numbers of users exploded upward. As a result, customer service saw more work come in at a very swift pace. The new head of the department brought it highly valuable experience with her arrival. Nevertheless, when she made her first report to me, I was interested that she nearly bowled me over with the enormous pile of papers she was carrying. She had been extremely conscientious in putting together a summary of all of the statistics and work reports on the customer service in the past. Then, based on the anticipated increase in business, she had prepared a plan for how to improve things in the future that ran to more than a dozen pages.

I spent an entire morning poring through all this with her. I then said, "You are a true expert on customer service. I am a complete novice. I have to say frankly that I do not totally understand all these tables and statistics you have put together. Since you are the expert, if you understand them, that is the important thing. But I wonder, would it be possible for us to do without KPIs? What if I gave you only one target? Get our young customer service staff to truly love this work, from the inside out?"

The question is, how do you get employees in customer service to emancipate their thinking and voluntarily provide excellent service? In the past, we mobilized everyone to study the famous Chinese hot pot restaurant named Hai Di Lao Hot Pot. As we know, employees actually smiled when they dealt with customers, and it was a sincere smile. They practically ran when they wiped down the tables. Hai Di Lao believed that you first had to create an environment of respect and trust for your own employees, before they could provide the same respect to their customers in a genuine way. Employees had to know that providing good service was doing a great job.

One small anecdote: An old man in Beijing, over 70, had a grandson who really liked Mi. He wanted to buy one for him as a birthday gift, but he didn't have an account with an online bank, much less any idea of how to purchase online. He therefore called our customer service number and asked what he should do. He said that he absolutely had to buy a phone for his grandson's birthday. One of our employees then went online to access her own bank account and put her own money down to buy the old man a phone. She put his address on the order form, so it would be sent straight to him. The old man was extremely grateful, and he immediately went to the customer service department to hand over the money. "I'm looking for that nice lady who loves customer service," he said. Colleagues asked her later, "What if he had been tricking you? What were you planning to do if you didn't get the money?" First, she said, her task was to resolve customers' problems. Second, she knew that the old man would not trick her. Third, if the old man did not repay the money, she knew her boss would not allow her to cover the cost alone.

All of the front-line staff members of our customer service personnel have a limited authority to present small gifts to customers in the course of helping them resolve problems. Employees do not have to ask their superiors for permission to do this. There are 1,800 customer service employees, and each can make his or her own determination about the user he or she is dealing with, whether or not he or she should extend a small token to that user to help facilitate the relationship. We have a system that tallies this kind of gifting activity in a simple way. It includes the cost of the gift and a general idea of why it was given. We do not go too deeply into the details, however. We believe that these first-line colleagues can make accurate and reasonable determinations according to specific circumstances. In fact, the more you have faith in them and lift restrictions, the more cautious and careful they are.

Trust is a major feature of the Xiaomi culture. When we were just starting to set up what we call Mi Homes, we delivered a load of goods to each of these places every three days. Each received a considerable number of phones, but at the end of the year we counted up the number that had been shipped and compared it against the inventory at these places. We had not lost a single one.

This kind of trust cannot be developed through any systems or KPIs.

We provide our service departments with considerable freedom. At the beginning, the people in charge of customer service were reluctant to embrace this concept. Those people with a great deal of experience were particularly unwilling to let go of control. Nevertheless, it worked. When we provided customer service managers with limited authority and gave them excellent remuneration, options, and trust when they proved to be outstanding, we received performance in return. Everyone in customer service began to feel that they were respected as much as the R&D people, even though they were mere "customer service workers."

We provide Xiaomi customer service teams with salaries that are 20 to 30 percent higher than the standard wage for the same job in the industry. In addition, they work in cubicles that are larger than the standard traditional customer service work station, and we provide all employees with the same quality of chairs, each of which costs several thousand RMB. What's more, after a person has worked for six months and performed well, he or she is granted options in the company. We have also set up the XiaomiAcademy for training grassroots-level personnel, to provide graduates with a professional skills certificate. All of this is to generate a sense of belonging among employees, to enable each grassroots-level customer service person to work in a way that shows to customers that he or she truly enjoys the work.

Our hope is to break out of the traditional attitude about customer service. The idea is to set up a progressive customer service system that is self-driven and that takes Xiaomi itself as the product. The key to this kind of system is people. How much priority you place on service is really decided by how much investment you put into service. I have said many times to colleagues in the customer service business that Xiaomi is a start-up and practices cost savings and frugality. We do not spend recklessly if there is no need to spend. However, with regard to service, we do not stint on the investment. In that arena, we are ready to spend.

Although customer service work does not directly bring revenue into the company, we regard money that is put into customer service as money that is invested in marketing and advertising. I believe that every penny put into our customer service will bring back a much greater return.

In the more than two years since 2013 and 2014, our attrition rate among the more than 100 managers of customer service teams has been less than 5 percent. This rate is unique among all industries that have customer service departments.

Xiaomi has another very special form of customer service, which is our fans themselves. Our products rely on word-of-mouth reputation, and the great majority of users that purchase the products had those products recommended to them by friends. More than 20 percent of users will loan their Xiaomi account number to friends to help them buy a product. When those users get into any kind of problem with the product, therefore, they will first go looking for their friend to ask him or her to help out. These highly senior fans will at that point become extremely useful in the extracurricular role of Xiaomi customer service personnel. The number of people in this group of customer service is vastly larger than any company could set up as a customer service department within its own ranks.

We value these fans tremendously. We constantly improve our product experience based on their responses to each generation of Mi. At the same time, we frequently hold activities to express appreciation to them, we give them preferential treatment so that they can be first to use new products, and we invite them to attend the product releases.

A customer strategy that "makes friends with users" and that employs the three-on-three principles of developing a sense of engagement helps employees also feel a sense of engagement. As always, it comes back to the importance of the human element. When you are confronted with systems, focus more on the human element. It will bring you much better returns.

Service Is the Credo of the Xiaomi Business Model

Why must Xiaomi emphasize service?

When I interview people for the job of managing customer service departments, I often tell them, "If your desire is to deliver good service, Xiaomi is a good place to work. The Xiaomi business model is like a restaurant model: you receive tips only if you have provided good service. Therefore you must provide excellent service."

Providing good service is not just the credo of the company and the boss, however. More importantly, it is the credo of the Xiaomi business model (Figure 5.2).

In setting up its business model, Xiaomi regards hardware products as the software of the Internet. Meanwhile, Internet software makes profits through oceans of volume and very slim margins. Companies that rely on "tips" to make their living will soon close down if they do not provide excellent service. As Lei Jun has repeatedly said to us in company meetings, "We have to be just that much better at making products and providing service, to get users to like us. When they like us and reward us with a tip, that's enough. What we need is that tip."

The Xiaomi business model is therefore what determines the fact that its core competitiveness lies with good service.

In traditional companies, customer service is not all that highly regarded. Many corporate leaders give it lip service, but in fact they pay low salaries to the people who actually do it. They put very little into the working environment of these people. What's more, customer service departments are generally regarded as a cost center. Many enterprises even look upon them as a kind of firewall in between the company and users—they are out there in front to take the brunt of criticism.

FIGURE 5.2 *Service is the credo of the Xiaomi business model.*

Customers therefore do indeed criticize. After finally reaching customer service departments, they get angry: "You talk a good line, but you don't actually do anything!"

From the very first day, Xiaomi took a different approach. We decided that adequate strategic investment had to go into customer service. We were faced with a major challenge, however, due to the way our sales volume increased so fast. What that meant was that we had to outsource a considerable amount of our customer servicing—at the beginning, 60 percent of positions were outsourced, and only 40 percent were in-house. Now we have gradually turned that around so that 75 percent are in-house, and 25 percent are outsourced. Still, we feel that is not enough. I hope that in the future 100 percent of our customer service personnel will be our own employees. Only when people are part of the company will they have a great sense of identification with the job—only then will they feel that they are providing service to their own customers.

If you emphasize service, you first must have good products. We require that each employee who works in customer service be a fan of Xiaomi products, just as the people do in our R&D team. They have to use their own products every day. We also encourage the idea of having fans become employees.

After experiencing the kind of service we provide at Mi Homes in person, many users apply to work with us. They say that the service is quite different in that it treats people like friends. It handles each case carefully and in an atmosphere that is positive and cheerful. The head of the Mi Home in Hangzhou was a fan before coming to work for us. His BBS identification was the famous West Wind. After entering the company, he quickly rose to be head of the store.

Provide Customer Service Wherever the Customer Is

How do you resolve customer problems quickly?

Wherever the customer may be, you should around him or her. Don't wait for the customer to come to you. You should go to the customer initiatively (Figure 5.3).

Many companies provide users with one channel for after-sales service—namely, a toll-free telephone number. But what if it is not convenient to make a phone call, or what if a problem comes up in the middle of the night? The user calls and gets an answering service: "Our work hours are from 9 a.m. in the morning to 6 p.m. at night." Most of us have probably had that experience. This traditional method of providing service is pretty much like telling users that they have to fit into the company's framework if they want any service at all.

Instead, Xiaomi provides service to the customers when and where they need it. Many of the most avid users of the company's products were born after 1990 and even after 2000—making a phone call is not the way they usually communicate. Instead, they go online. Because of this, we have a 24/7 customer service platform online.

At the beginning, in 2010, Xiaomi operated customer service only on its BBSs. Starting with the BBSs for the MIUI, when we had only a few dozen employees, everyone, including software engineers and founders,

FIGURE 5.3 *Provide service wherever the customer is.*

would respond to user questions on the BBS. As the number of users increased, we set up a special section on the BBS to receive inquiries from customers and resolve every one of the problems that came up in customer feedback.

After Xiaomi released the first smartphone in 2011, we set up a toll-free telephone number type of customer service system as well as an online customer service system. Still later, when many of our users were on Weibo, we set up a service on Weibo that handled inquiries about how to use MIUI and to provide feedback on how to use Mi. We set up a team with several dozen people that communicated on Weibo directly on a one-to-one basis with users. Every day, many tens of thousands of people would go through Weibo to send private messages or critiques to Xiaomi, and we were able to respond to each of these user issues within 15 minutes. Once WeChat became extremely popular, we then set up a dedicated operating team for customer service just on WeChat. In the same fashion, we also began to handle direct customer service users on Baidu Zhidao and Baidu Tieba, in order to service users on the Baidu platform.

It might help to explain how we provide customer service on Weibo more specifically. First, we have an auxiliary platform. We developed a customer service platform that directly links in to Weibo because otherwise it would be hard to handle so many users and service their needs in such a short amount of time. Second, we constantly improve upon our response time overall. At the outset, it was 30 minutes, and now we have it down to 15 minutes. Third, with respect to language, we explain clearly as much as possible. On Weibo, we even make jokes with customers. Because many of the messages coming in on Weibo are private messages, we can treat customers as our friends.

Let Service Centers Be Just Like Home

The person in charge of after-sales servicing for Xiaomi once came to me with a question: "How much should we spend on tables, and how much on wall lamps? What's the allocation?" I asked a question in return: "When you decorate your own home, do you think about KPIs?" (Figure 5.4).

That was in 2013. We had decided to upgrade the concept of what we call Mi Homes. We were closing places that were too small and instead were putting all our efforts into making flagship stores that could serve as model examples of this customer service. This included supporting authorized after-sales service locations that were doing a good job. The person in charge had therefore come to me with this question.

After that, as she was remodeling one of these places, she changed the product display tables four times!

Mi Homes are official service flagship stores that provide after-sales service, as well as the actual experience of products. They serve as locations where the company can interact with users. Unlike other after-sales stores, our intent is to make them as comfortable and as much like "home" as possible.

FIGURE 5.4 *Let service centers be just like home.*

We opted for many untraditional ways of doing things in launching this initiative. Generally speaking, it is hard to set up an after-sales service network on a nationwide basis if you are a new company and just in the start-up phase. In fact, doing so is a monumental task. The traditional, fast approach is to use a third-party network and authorize it to provide servicing on your behalf. Instead, we opted for what might be thought of as a foolish plan: in addition to launching service via a third-party network, we also simultaneously began to set up our own post-sales servicing stores, which we called Mi Homes. We did not locate these on busy streets. Instead, we chose places in office buildings, away from the noise and the hubbub, but we required that they be easily accessed by public transportation. For example, they had to be within a 10-minute walk of a subway station. Meanwhile, even though these were service stations, their interiors had to be designed so as to make them just as attractive as a sales outlet.

The defining intentions of a Mi Home were "experience" and "service," not sales (Figure 5.5). Say a user had just purchased a Xiaomi product, or say there was a potential customer who had not yet purchased anything. When this person entered a Mi Home, he would find a wealth of things to do. He could directly experience new products, get his phone problem fixed, or ask Xiaomi attendants to help with upgrading or installing new systems. All of these things went without saying. In addition, he could hold a birthday party in the place, when it was raining he could borrow an umbrella, he could access the Internet for free, and he could even use the printer in Mi Homes to print out his thesis.

The launch of Mi Homes came after the August 16, 2011, release of the Mi. The people in charge of post-sales servicing traveled to seven cities within the space of 10 days, and they evaluated no fewer than 30 potential locations in each city. They then selected sites and signed rental contracts. At the same time, we hired both the heads of each service location and employees to staff these sites from among local people. After another month of designing and outfitting, we had seven Mi Homes up and ready by the time phones were shipped out on a national basis, which was in November.

In achieving this, we owe a great deal to our local Mi Fans, and we would like to thank them. They helped us with advance arrangements, setting up places to see, and accompanying our team as they looked over places. It would have been impossible to do all this in 10 days without them. Indeed, the way they helped us as friends made us even more determined to set up Xiaomi service stations to help them in return.

From the outset, we designed the interiors of Mi Homes as though they were a person's own home. Users had been accustomed to service stations that were quite different—dim light, a counter separating the employees from users, a long row of plastic white chairs in which to wait. One by one, users would go up to the counter to present their problems. When users first came into a Mi Home, they found a totally new after-sales service environment.

Because of this, the Mi Homes have become the single most important window through which the company interacts with users. Not only are the places good looking, and not only do they have a comfortable

FIGURE 5.5 *Mi Homes*

and inviting atmosphere, but they also provide a wealth of services and activities. In the past two or more years, hundreds of thousands of fans nationwide have established close relationships with Xiaomi via its service center homes.

A small example: The Women's Day is held every March 18 in China, and on this day women who come to Mi Homes discover that they are greeted not only with the smiling faces of the staffs but also with fresh flowers prepared especially for them.

Another example: Since November 16, 2012, the festival that falls on the twenty-third or twenty-fourth of the twelfth month of the lunar year, Mi Homes invites Mi Fans who are unable to return to their homes to come in and have an evening meal together. Sitting around the table and eating dumplings and hot pot, Mi Homes truly becomes the home for Mi Fans.

I have been wondering about the feasibility of a fairly crazy idea: what if Mi Homes could have their own unique style and themes the way certain coffee shops do? After all, homes are all unique—they are not homogeneous and neatly identical to one another.

The Bit-by-Bit System

The idea of turning post-sales service centers into homes was a substantial innovation, which could be seen as an important innovation. But most of the services offered by Xiaomi fall into the category of micro-innovations.

Each time we open a Mi Home, we celebrate with millet porridge. When the Wuhan facility opened, they sent me a photograph that I greatly enjoyed—on top of the millet porridge, they had drawn an image that was like the swirl of whipped cream on top of a cappuccino, only this was in the shape of our Xiaomi logo.

One of our employees mentioned to me that he would like to enable users to come into a Mi Home and sense a new atmosphere each time. To that end, we provided each facility with incense burners and different kinds of incense. We found that the fragrance really did improve people's moods when they were having their phones serviced. This was an excellent micro-innovation.

For company employees, we have a special channel for repairs. When trial versions of phones that people are using run into problems, they take them to Mi Homes for repair. One day, a colleague in our sales department was very excited to tell me about her experience in this regard. When she dropped her phone and broke the screen, she took it to a Mi Home where a colleague replaced it for her. In addition, however, he pasted a thin film on it and, most importantly, placed her phone in an exquisitely made gift box and had it delivered back to her desk.

The constant improvements that are made in the quality of service come from recommendations of the front-line staffs. In order to sustain this kind of ongoing improvement, we decided to develop a product that we call the *bit-by-bit system*.

This actually is an app developed specifically for phones. Our service system personnel can recommend their own ideas through this bit-by-bit system. Everybody can see the recommendations that others put forth as well, in addition to people's critiques of ideas. Everyone can "suggest," "comment," "grade," and "like." We set up a five-person team specifically to handle this. They are responsible for publicizing the recommendations of front-line staffs, for comparing evaluations and presenting awards, and for implementing results. Good recommendations do not need to go through any meeting process. They can be directly passed on as long as three people on the operations team agree to it. This means that the recommendations can be adopted and implemented and become actual work procedures with minimal delay.

This innovation has been very effective in stimulating a positive work attitude among front-line staffs. As soon as a person's recommendation is adopted, he or she is given various incentive awards, including of course a Mitu but also including various accessories. The entire process is transparent to everyone in the company. Everyone therefore has a profound sense that the growth of the company is indeed due to their own intelligence, to the accumulation of their own efforts bit by bit.

The kind of interaction based on service also heightens the sense of engagement.

Speed Is of the Essence in Providing Good Service

Speed defeats anything.

The Xiaomi brand name applies to the company's service as much as it does to anything else. Seven words to describe four concepts: focus, ultimate excellence, word-of-mouth reputation, speed. What is the fundamental need of users when it comes to service? It is speed. They want fast delivery of goods, fast response time on inquiries, and fast resolution of post-sales problems.

With respect to fast delivery of goods, Xiaomi has established a 24-hour-delivery-time system in core cities. It has signed contracts with logistics companies for service upgrades and customized delivery services. It has made improvements in the dispatching of products from warehouses, and it has set up more central warehouses—going from 6 to 10. In selecting delivery service companies, we make decisions based on speed (Figure 5.6). Cost is a secondary consideration.

FIGURE 5.6 *Speed is of the essence in providing good service.*

On November 11, 2013, during the Double Eleventh event conducted via Tmall, the Xiaomi logistics center processed 180,000 orders, a record at the time. By April 8, 2014, during the Mi Fans Festival, this number had gone up by three times, to 560,000.

The speed at which Xiaomi set up post-sales service departments has rarely if ever been seen in the industry. Starting in July 2011, in addition to establishing 7 Mi Homes nationwide—finding the locations, renovating the space, hiring people, training them, plus a host of other things—Xiaomi also completed the setup for a network alliance of 300 other post-sales service locations. By April 2014, we had increased this figure to 500 locations, plus 18 Mi Homes. We had also implemented a service that was first in the industry, called "One-hour service or else we pay a fine."

If service is not done to satisfaction within one hour, Xiaomi will pay the user a voucher for RMB 20. That is, in order to have the user feel that the service really is "fast," we promise that no more than one hour will go by from the time the user presents his or her complaint at the front counter to the time the service is complete. In addition, we started an on-site game of throwing large dice—if the service is not completed on time, the user gets a cash coupon for RMB 20, with which to play this game of throwing dice (Figure 5.7). Depending on what he or she is

FIGURE 5.7 *Users who wait longer than an hour get to play the game of throwing dice.*

able to hit, he or she can draw different small prizes. All of this is a way of apologizing for not keeping our promise of getting the job done on time. The result has been that the normally grim atmosphere in which people wait for repairs to be finished has turned into a more relaxed and enjoyable scene.

The Xiaomi customer service department had only a few dozen people when it started out. By June 2014, the department encompassed a team of 1,800 people, including those providing service via telephone and online. In addition, Xiaomi was the first in the country to provide 24/7 service. In order to provide fast solutions to user feedback, we also set up service platforms on Weibo, WeChat, Qzone, Baidu Zhidao, and Baidu Tieba, among others. We respond to post-sales requests almost immediately. For example, if the customer sends a private message to Xiaomi on Weibo, we will respond in 15 minutes.

As a form of company culture, speed has also infiltrated the practices of the more than 500 authorized service agents that Xiaomi uses. They have also opened their own Weibo and WeChat addresses. The peak hour for usage on Weibo is 9 p.m., and our agents have set up special personnel to be available at this time to search key words relating to Xiaomi and their local post-sales issues so as to be able to respond to requests as fast as possible.

Speed can become a form of core competitiveness in customer servicing. Handling the customer service needs for a smartphone business has been like building the Great Wall, and it has a very long chain. In its first three years, Xiaomi created the framework for speed; then in 2014, it required higher-quality service from its logistical systems and its post-sales customer service operations. Reaching this step required adequate funding in addition to simple determination. This related to what Lei Jun has always regarded as essential for a start-up's success: choose a business with a large market, find a superlative team, and make sure you have plenty of money.

It is pointless to talk about such things as personalized service and differentiated service if your products are not delivered fast enough and customer inquiries are not answered fast enough. If you want to get to the root of good service, the central issue is simply speed.

Go Above and Beyond the Usual Standard Service

Nobody likes an artificial smile.

Sincerity is the most important thing when it comes to whether or not people feel good about your service.

Traditional customer service involves training staff to respond to inquiries with standardized responses. In the Xiaomi servicing systems, not only do we make sure that service personnel have those conventional responses in hand but we also ask that they forget those responses when appropriate. We ask them to explain solutions as clearly as possible in the face of specific problems (Figure 5.8).

The reason is that our service people are dealing with human beings. Customers cannot feel good if you turn service staff into machines by drilling them to give standardized responses and then ask these machines to talk to people.

At the outset, this approach made a lot of traditional customer service staff feel uneasy. Asking them to use nonstandardized language to respond

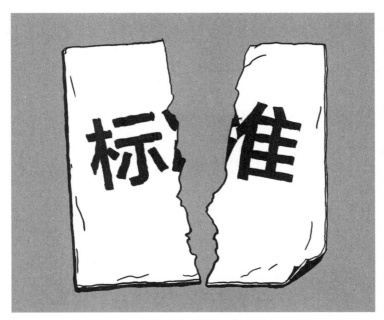

FIGURE 5.8 *Go above and beyond the usual standard service.*

to users made them afraid of saying the wrong thing. We handled this by having them listen to tapes every day of responses to customers' inquiries. We then asked them to evaluate whether those responses were good or not, and how to improve them by changing this or that sentence. Every day they would make small changes—all customer service staff participated in this process of improvement. We found that what we changed was not just rote responses but also the whole approach to communicating with customers (Figure 5.9).

At Mi Homes, we often say that this approach of providing unconventional service means doing things with their hearts. A small example: One time a user came to the Mi Home in Suzhou with a phone that needed repair. It was obvious she was not in a good mood. Our staff therefore gave her a hand-painted phone shell, so that her phone now

---

PRODUCT EVALUATIONS

Customer:
It's ok, but the cord does not feel secure

Xiaomi Customer Service:
Hello. Our earphones are made to be placed inside the ear. You might try adjusting the angle as you put the earphone securely in your ear. Believe me, once you get it in your ear the results will be better. Thank you for your support.

✴ ✴ ✴ ✴ ✴ *(From evaluation #179538941 on April 16, 2014)*

Customer:
Fantastic quality! Terrific sound.

Xiaomi Customer Service:
Hello. We can see at a glance that you are from the northeast—we are both straightforward types. Thank you for your support.

✴ ✴ ✴ ✴ ✴ *(From evaluation #96291915 on April 16, 2014)*

Customer:
The sound quality is really quite good. I even washed it in the washing machine twice by accident and the sound was not affected.

Xiaomi Customer Service:
Hello. Our products are quite trustworthy, but I have to compliment you in return—you really are able to handle a lot. Thank you for your support.

✴ ✴ ✴ ✴ ✴ *(From evaluation #160898388 on April 16, 2014)*

Customer:
Good good good. Number One in the entire world—keep it up Xiaomi!

Xiaomi Customer Service:
Hello. It is because of support like yours that we not only want to be first in the world, but we want to beat out the competition. Please take care of yourself so you can see the day we are first in the universe. Thank you for your support.

✴ ✴ ✴ ✴ ✴ *(From evaluation #9891730 on April 16, 2014)*

Customer:
Bought it for my girlfriend, and she is a pretty powerful lady.

Xiaomi Customer Service:
Hello. This product is made precisely for such legendary goddesses. Thank you for your support.

✴ ✴ ✴ ✴ ✴ *(From evaluation #185588177 on April 16, 2014)*

FIGURE 5.9 *The Reply from Customer Service*

had a green tree on the back cover. Delighted, she said it was such a work of art that she wasn't going to use it. She was going to take it home and mount it on her wall as a work of art. Just before leaving, she even gave our staff a small gift in return.

In many companies, the customer service staff has no interaction at all with the business departments of the company. Generally they assemble the user feedback they have received into a report, which they hand over to the relevant department, and that's about it. In Xiaomi, we have always had the customer service department work together with our R&D staffs in the same location. If the telephone load suddenly goes up, the person in charge of customer service can immediately find the person responsible for the relevant product and find a direct way to answer questions.

The essence of the nonstandard service is that customers are more important than the system.

People Are the Children of Their Environment

A good restaurant depends on its kitchen, and a good service center depends on its storeroom.

In a storeroom, spare parts and accessories are kept for post-sales repair work. In visiting the internal warehouses of other companies in their service centers, we discovered that they are built simply to satisfy functional needs. The front counter of a service center is always very attractive while the storeroom looks primitive by comparison. Mi Homes were the same at the beginning.

I believe that people are the children of their environment (Figure 5.10). Customer service personnel will treat customers as "work that must be done" if their own environment is not conducive to better treatment. Because of this, Xiaomi puts the same careful attention on the environment for staff as it does for customers. This includes the back-office part of Mi Homes.

All of us may well think it is all right to spit on the ground when we are outdoors in some wild place. When we have a suit and tie on

FIGURE 5.10 *People are the children of their environment.*

and are walking down the red carpet, naturally we wouldn't dream of doing this. Environments give people signals, and people behave accordingly. At Mi Homes, our service staff members wear youthful T-shirts all day, or at least young-looking clothes, which makes them much more inclined to have a spontaneous and youthful approach to customers. You find them smiling much more readily. You simply do not see the kind of situation one often encounters in the usual post-sales repair centers—customers looking worried, staff looking grim and just trying to do their best as they follow prescribed procedures. Service that is regulated through a rigid system is a false-hearted kind of service, while that which is generated through a beneficial environment is genuine.

Xiaomi requires that its storeroom in Mi Homes not only be clean and tidy but also aesthetically pleasing. Although these places are not open to the public, they are where staff must work every single day. It is important to equip them not only with attractive racks and boxes but also with green plants and coffee machines. The point is to make every person who works at a Mi Home feel good about working there.

Making staff happy is not just a matter of providing better benefits—it's not that simple. When employees are working in a place that is comfortable and attractive, in which there is a changing room specifically for them and even a well-designed coffee pot, in which everything is orderly, bright, and appealing, employees will instinctively feel that they are doing a job that requires this kind of quality.

Xiaomi provides its front-line service staff with a clean and orderly work environment, which allows them, on a daily basis, to feel the existence of beauty. What's more, as people continue to work in such an environment over time, they unconsciously begin to cultivate good habits and begin to take care of their own surroundings themselves. When people change shifts at Mi Homes, they consciously make things look nice for the next team. They straighten up their chairs and clean up before leaving work.

A lot of companies provide their own employees with an internal online office system. The fact is, however, that these internal office systems are often not that great; plus they have an ugly interface. We generally reject these systems—not only are they hard to learn but also, once employees have learned them, it is harder for them to change.

Instead, our question to ourselves is, why can't we use the thinking behind cutting-edge products to create our own back-office systems?

Why not change our back-office systems the minute we find they aren't working right, and revise them in an ASAP manner?

Because of this thinking, our back-office systems for service are also updated weekly, just as is our MIUI.

One example is our internal F Code issuing system. At the beginning, the F Codes were coded by an engineer. They were then issued to the relevant colleague by keying the code individually into a computer. The colleague then distributed them out to the "friends." As the number of employees kept increasing, however, this work became more and more of a hassle. The engineers for our database center back-office systems then decided to create a back-office system for issuing F Codes that met everyone's needs.

At first, they just made a simple product, a location on the website. After entering the employees' account system, the employees could use their own company account to get the approved number of F Codes on their own. Colleagues in the marketing department then wanted this system too: "In our marketing operations, we need to apply for F Codes as well—can you add this function to the system?" In no time at all, the engineers had developed a back-office system for applying for codes and getting permission for them. When it appeared that this might create security problems, they then developed a system that incorporated cell phone numbers for security.

Although this was an internal system with only some few thousand users, our back-office development team was still attentive to all feedback and suggestions offered by those who were receiving the F Codes. They continued to make constant improvements and to upgrade the system. By now, this system can handle applications for F Codes and issue them to users, and it can also, at the same time, distribute all kinds of coupon codes for products that can be obtained internally by employees as a part of their benefits. Not only can employees apply online but they can also use a cell phone app that our team developed. At any time and any place, employees can look things up, apply, and use a whole variety of coupon codes. This, meanwhile, is just one of the dozens of internal back-office systems that our back-office systems team has developed.

Our reasons for doing this: First, we wanted to improve work efficiency. Second, again, we realized that people are the product of their environment. The kind of office environment that you provide to your employees determines the work results that they provide in return. The feelings that employees intuit about the way the company respects their service has a direct impact on the attitude with which they themselves provide service to customers.

CHAPTER 6

DESIGN

Hit the Nail on the Head

"Hit the nail on the head" sums up Xiaomi's thinking about design.

In concrete terms, this means that all documentation that goes with products and also our general way of expressing things has to meet two design requirements. First, it must be direct, use common language, and allow the user to understand at once. Second, it has to hit the essential points, be intuitively understandable, and make an impact on the user (Figure 6.1).

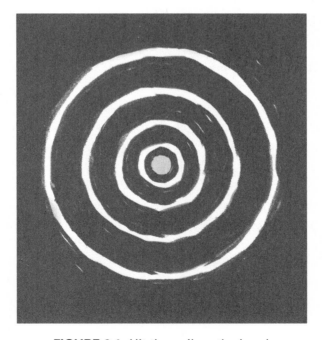

FIGURE 6.1 *Hit the nail on the head.*

The phrase one sees most often in advertisements these days is "outstanding and uncommon." In the design process in Xiaomi, this is also the term that we most ridicule. I often remind staff that the products are recommended to others and sold by word-to-mouth reputation. When we define selling points for the products, therefore, all we really need to think about is one scenario: How would you recommend the product to your friends? You certainly would not say things like, "Mi is really outstanding and uncommon." Instead, you might say, "Mi is fast enough" (Figure 6.2).

FIGURE 6.2 *The Alternative Poster of "Mi Is Fast Enough"*

Colleagues suggest many marketing plans to me for consideration. My first response often is, "Don't make it so convoluted. Can you be simpler and more direct?" The trap many companies fall into in terms of design is to be too abstract or arrogant. All of these things sound fine, and they seem cool enough to improve the level of your brand. Because they can be used anywhere, for anything, they do not grab hold of any essential point. The second pitfall companies fall into is that they often mistakenly think that catchwords are selling points. They do not focus on the greatest aspect of their product or clarify the most essential thing.

Here is how Xiaomi approaches the mass advertising of some its products—this may help clarify the concept.

Case 1. "Mi Is Fast Enough"

After the Mi 2 was released, we prepared to put out a mass-market ad that set the scene for the product. The core selling point of Mi 2 was that it had many times the number of functions. It was the first smartphone with a quad core ever to be produced and sold anywhere in the world. We therefore were inclined to focus on the unique feature of high functionality in our ad, with "fast" being a key. Our designers wrote many advertising slogans, such as "speed is unbreakable" and "excellent functions like a wild beast." In the end we chose, "Mi is fast enough" (Figure 6.3). This was to the point, and it used plain language.

FIGURE 6.3 *The Final Poster of "Mi Is Fast Enough"*

Advertising transmits information by using coded language, which consumers then need to decode. In the course of this transmission, there is always noise interference and information loss. The most effective coding is easy to code and decode. It preserves the greatest degree of authenticity.

Case 2. RMB 99 Headphones

This is the story of the ad copy for the Mi headphones device product (Figure 6.4). Marketing earphone devices is difficult because the product is so specialized. For example, you need to talk about the quality of sound, but that is something that images and words can't describe accurately. We looked over essentially all of the marketing tricks used by other earphone makers, and we discovered that the ads were exaggerated. They all talked about "prominent high-frequency, stable midfrequency, and powerful low-frequency resonance." Since this was the first time Xiaomi was putting out an earphone device, if it used the same approach, it would not stand out from the others, and it would probably not be as professional as the others either.

FIGURE 6.4 *The Poster of Mi Piston Headphones*

Design and planning have to use the product as the starting point. Our starting point was that this was a device aimed at mass-market appeal. It was not of such ultimate quality that professionals would want to use it. Instead, it provided the great majority of users with quite adequate sound, enough that they would first think of Xiaomi if they wanted to purchase quality-assured headphones. More specifically, it was what they would choose if they wanted something that would beat out others in the range of alternatives on the market that were priced between RMB 200 and 500.

In the end, the product we came out with did indeed lead the field in this price range, but we set our price at RMB 99. High-end users are not much interested in this range of products. One Internet expert on earphone devices noted, "This earphone device is not fantastic—in my opinion it is worth RMB 300 at the most." In fact, this was an excellent third-party confirmation of the quality of our product. It set the value at RMB 300 for Mi headphones.

As our planning team dissected the selling points of this product, they also at the same time considered what name to give it.

We had a new person handling the planning for this product at the time. He came out of an advertising company and brought with him some conventional ideas about how to write ad copy. He started out by producing a whole pile of suggestions that all included the term "spirit / intelligence." I thought these were similar to every other product on the street, and so they were absolutely unable to differentiate our brand. We needed something simpler and more direct. We found a solution in the shape of the sound box, the speaker unit's exterior, which was like a piston. We therefore gave the product the name Mi Piston Headphones, which also gave people a sense of dynamic action.

Product points can be divided into selling points and stunts. Selling points are what make the users pull out their money to pay for something. Stunts are fun, but they are not enough to make people pay for them. We also divide selling points into two grades: first grade and second grade. There can only be one item in a first grade selling point since it has to be memorable to users. If you throw in three or four, the users can't remember them all, and you might as well have none. Second grade selling points provide a supplementary description, and we generally use two or three.

How were we going to come up with a first grade selling point for the Mi Piston Headphones? Our product team on this product had first-class experience in the supply chain of the product and the workmanship that went into its manufacturing. We thought of improving the technology to improve the tone quality. The key thing we wanted to transmit to users was a sense of quality. We included three aspects: technology, material, and packaging.

With respect to technology, we particularly wanted to mention that this sound box was cast from one piece of aluminum. In terms of material, we wanted to mention that we used Kevlar wire of for military grade. As for the third selling point, our planning colleagues wanted to mention the multicolored winder. Many people had not used the product yet, however, and they would not understand what that referred to, so in the end we opted for wording about how the product came wrapped in "high-quality packaging for gift giving." That thereby included the cord-coiling device and the exquisitely manufactured box. Here is a list of the candidate phrases we finally came up with:

- First grade selling point 1: "Inspiration comes from the design of the F1 piston."
  This was rejected. It was too abstract.
- First grade selling point 2: "The sound chamber is made from an aeronautic aluminum alloy in one piece."
  This was rejected. It was more like a second grade selling point.
- Second grade selling point 1: "The material was like a pacifier…, soft, and comfortable."
  This was rejected. This was not a selling point. It was more like a stunt.

We finally decided upon a selling point: "Mi Piston Headphones, only RMB 99 but high quality."

We did not say "listening music" because that sounded too professional. It also lacked the warmth of "songs." We used an unprecedented price-to-features ratio, and we were able to sell headphones valued at RMB 300, given materials, technology, and appearance, at a mere RMB 99. The planning team selected the term "miracle device."

We started out with 12 selling points for the headphones. These later were reduced to 7, and as more were rejected, they went down to a remaining 3. The process was one of subtracting everything extraneous and going for simplicity. In fact, our methodology was even simpler: it involved just thinking of how we would recommend the product to our own friends. We certainly would not adorn our recommendation with the kind of language used in ads. Instead, we would note the most important factors in a straightforward way: "The sound chamber is made out of aeronautic aluminum alloy in one piece," which meant the tone quality was good. "Kevlar wire designed for military use" meant that the materials were good. "The high-quality packaging for gift giving is included in the RMB 99," when you could spend that much on the box alone. In fact, everyone who saw the product found it very easy to remember these three key selling points. Some people used just one standard way of recommending the product to their friends, however—they would point to the Kevlar wire.

I have always maintained that you must not use a lot of empty rhetoric in trying to market your product. Say the things that are most meaningful to your users, and say them in the simplest and most direct way. That's enough.

Case 3. 10,400 mAh Mi Power Bank, RMB 69

This is a case study about the product descriptions of the 10,400 milliampere hours (mAh) Mi power bank (Figure 6.5).

At the outset, our planning team wanted to describe this product in terms of its small size and enormous capacity. They also wanted to emphasize the fact that the 10,400 mAh could power the phone for a long time. There were also some other descriptions that condensed these things, such as, "Not just powerful but long-lasting," but these were rejected.

- Version 1. "Small in size, large in capacity"
  This was rejected. It was too abstract—that is, it was not intuitively understandable. For example, one had to wonder just how small or how big something was, which made one think again.

FIGURE 6.5 *The Poster of the Mi Power Bank*

- Version 2. "Redefines the concept of power bank"
  This was rejected. It was too abstract. In a fundamental sense, we had not done any redefining, and this made it too easy for us to be criticized.
- Version 3. "Unimaginably exciting"
  This was rejected. It fell in the premier class, without conveying any essential point.
- Version 4. "The smartphone companion with the best cost performance"
  This was rejected. It was too indirect because no one had any idea what the product was used for—the first thing users think of as a smart phone "companion" is Wi-Fi.
- Version 5. "Small enough to hold in one hand, sufficiently powered for a whole day"
  This was rejected. "Sufficiently powered for a whole day" does not provide any point of differentiation.
- Version 6. "The most suitable accessory to Mi"
  This was rejected. "Accessory" is not specific enough, and it generally refers to a phone shell.

- Version 7. "Magical charger device that costs only RMB 69"
  This was rejected. "Magical device" had already been used by the Redmi and the Mi Piston Headphones. Using it again was a lazy way of doing things, and so we rejected it on principle.

Considering all of these, in the end I said, "Let's just say outright what the size is and what the price is. That is the most direct of all." So we decided on the following first grade selling point: "10,400 mAh, RMB 69." For the second grade selling point, we chose this: "International chip used in LG and Samsung, shell with aluminum alloy."

At that time, the market for power banks was chaotic, with other brands with the same capacity being priced at around RMB 150. What's more, the other brands' shells were made of plastic. The chip and circuits were as simple as possible, and they didn't have any kind of design. It was therefore best to talk about the most obvious things: with 10,400 mAh, the Mi power bank was only RMB 69. This kind of cost performance was crazy. If users showed interest, we followed that up with even more:

it had a chip used in LG and Samsung products, it had circuits used in Texas Instruments, and it had a shell that was aluminum alloy in one piece, the same as the Apple MacBook.

Design Also Has to Hit the Nail on the Head

After looking at a number of design ideas and talking over the overall look and shape, we decided that the design also had to hit the nail on the head. My feeling is that the best digital products are not too ostentatious in design. The main thing is that the design has to show quality—it has to make the users want to own it.

As for the ad campaign for the phone, the designer first presented the idea of a jaguar pouncing out of the screen of the phone. This was to go along with the wording "Mi is fast enough." This looked cool, but it made the phone become secondary. We could not take up the idea because the "star" of the product had to be the phone itself.

We put a lot of thought into how to display the product itself, from what angle, with what composition. The first version of the poster for the power bank viewed it from the side, which looked marvelous, but in the end we decided against it and opted to have a frontal view with someone holding it. The reason was that we wanted to let users know that the product also felt good. This was in addition to its other excellent qualities—high-cost performance, sturdy materials, outstanding design, and good feeling to hand-hold.

Finally, the framework in which we present information in posters is also critical. Our general approach is to present things from the top down: the first sentence is the first grade selling point; the following are second grade selling points, price, then an image of the product, the Internet site where you can buy it, and the company logo. Putting the price in a prominent position is a key feature in Xiaomi because our trademark is a high-cost performance.

Nobody Likes Plastic Flowers—Only Real Flowers Move People

Nobody likes plastic flowers. Our design had to have temperature to it. It had to move people. It had to have emotional appeal, and this meant that the design had to make special efforts to achieve two things. First, it had to consider design from the standpoint of how the product was defined. Second, it had to use classic scenes from either daily life or what we call a "holiday culture" (Figure 6.6).

FIGURE 6.6 *Nobody likes plastic flowers— only real flowers move people.*

Case 1. The Very First Television Bought by Young People
When we made the Mi TV, our intent was to make a product that young people could afford.

In defining the functions of this product, we first reviewed the size of televisions in the market and thought about how big ours should be. Young people do not live in mansions. The living room of their first independent home generally has 100- to 120-square feet to accommodate a TV. Because of that, we opted for a screen that was 47 inches wide. That put our product within the mainstream category in terms of size. At the same time, though, it allowed us to select the best components while also keeping the price within RMB 3,000. Other companies in the industry were selling televisions at over RMB 6,000. We then took younger people into account in designing the actual look of the product by deciding to make it in different colors.

At the product release, we were faced with a challenging issue. If we exhibited the television in the usual fashion, in a large sales room, it would look small. If, on the other hand, we lined up televisions in rows the way other companies did, it would look messy, squeezed, and ordinary. It would lose any sense of being a quality product.

In the end, we decided to make sample rooms to resemble the ways in which the televisions might actually be placed in someone's home (Figure 6.7). We had one that was artistic, one that was commercial, one that was for indie pop, and one for rock. Our design team selected furniture with exquisite attention to what people would actually put in their rooms. They took color cards with them to match up just the right colors to go with the various colors of our Mi TV, and they had to turn the entire IKEA store upside down in the process.

Our overall design concept addressed the questions, "What is the size of my room?" "What kind of person am I?" "What type of place do I live in?" "What type of TV do I need?" On the day we made the presentation, not only were users and the media astonished but our design team itself was also bowled over by the results. One of our R&D engineers told me that as he was on his way to the presentation, he wondered what we might come up with. Once he saw the way we exhibited the experience of the product, he was absolutely shocked. It was beyond what he could have imagined.

After the physical display was ended, we moved these rooms to our official product website and onto the purchasing site for television sets, in order to enable more users to have a sense of engagement. They could start their own creative process of thinking how to decorate their new homes, and they could match up their own design sense with just the right color of television set. What's more, after designing their rooms, they could show off their unique approach to using their Mi TV set on Weibo. From viewing to creating to sharing, the idea of "Showing off my living room" quickly generated a positive response from more than a million users. We told users that what they were selecting was not just a television set but also a lifestyle that belonged specifically to them.

A true story: After buying a Mi TV set, one of our users eventually changed the entire look of her home to suit a new self-image. She first

FIGURE 6.7 *The Sample Rooms of Mi TV*

changed the rack where she put the set, then she repainted the walls, then she changed the rest of the furniture. The Mi TV set inspired her to make changes in line with what she aspired to be, and she changed her living environment as a result.

Case 2. A Holiday Culture

The initial launches of two of our products, the Mi Wi-Fi and the 5,200 mAh Mi Power Bank, were timed to take advantage of two holidays: New Year's and Valentine's Day (Figure 6.8). We therefore looked for aspects of the products that could resonate with the public mood so as to amplify the "chemical reaction" in an unusual way.

FIGURE 6.8 *The Mi Wi-Fi Launch on New Year's Day*

The prelaunch "warming-up period" for the Mi Wi-Fi corresponded perfectly with Christmas. We created Anytime Wi-Fi in six colors, and we gave each one a distinctive tune. These were accessible on the website page of the product in short segments. The users could either activate them with their mouse or with keystrokes on the keyboard—each color linked in to the corresponding segment of the tune. The tune that we chose was "Jingle Bells," divided into two segments. We put the product page online on Christmas Eve. The users could play the tunes, and the USB icon would appear with the Mi Wi-Fi in the corresponding color, which strengthened the emotional element of the visual. In the end, 1.2 million users played the tune through to the end, which set a record for being the greatest number of users ever to play this famous music in one day in the world.

The time frame for the launch of the 5,200 mAh Mi Power Bank was short—just three days. Nevertheless, we had long since "buttoned up" Valentine's Day as being the right holiday for this product (Figure 6.9). Our design plan incorporated a vote for "the lady friend from whom you get the most electricity!" As Valentine's Day approached, we therefore took advantage of it by using the most appropriate concept for that event—namely, the match between a boy and a girl. We personified the 10,400 mAh Mi Power Bank as "male" and the 5,200 mAh Mi Power Bank as "female."

From a product perspective, the 10,400 mAh version was indeed used more by males because their hands were larger and they could install the power bank with one hand. Women found it easier to use the 5,200 mAh version. What's more, the pronunciation of "5,200" in Chinese somewhat resembles the sound of the words "I love you."

Design Has to Impart a Sense of Expectation

How do you build a sense of engagement into mass-market advertising?

Traditional Chinese painting has always emphasized to "leave enough white to hold the black." Design too must allow for sufficient empty space, in both visuals and language. It cannot be too wordy, which means it has to allow space for the imagination. It has to engender a sense of expectation (Figure 6.10). The three-on-three principles for developing a sense of engagement incorporate an interactive mode of engagement into the design process. Leaving space in which users can participate makes it easier for them to "come in" and express their own ideas.

FIGURE 6.9 *Mi Power Bank Launched on Valentine's Day*

The advance mass-market advertising for our new product releases is always a reflection of this classic aesthetic balance in the Xiaomi way of thinking about design.

We released the Mi 2 at the annual press conference in August 2012. We had sold over 1.5 million. This record for long-term sales will enter

FIGURE 6.10 *Design has to impart a sense of expectation.*

the annals of smart devices made in China. The performance of Mi 1 had enabled the company to stand firm and move forward. The launch of the Mi 2, on August 16, capitalized on the successes of that initial battle (Figure 6.11).

In designing the ad material for the launch, we wanted to use the tremendous enthusiasm of our user groups for Xiaomi products and the

FIGURE 6.11 *The Press Conference on August 16, 2012*

particular attributes of the fans. These things included a lot of technical factors as well as emotive design elements. The design team came up with a number of proposals. A large percentage of them had a problem, however, which was that they left too little white space, and thus too little room for the imagination.

What we did then was to separate out and evaluate the core information points about the product. In fact, this was the most fundamental part of design work and also the hardest step. We figured out that what we wanted to tell users was that the product being launched was a second-generation product, it had twice the functionality of the first generation, the date of its launch was August 16, and the place of its launch was the famous Dashanzi Art District in Beijing.

Once we had written these core elements out on the blackboard, the entire design team sat on the floor of the office in a group and revisited the whole concept. I began to wonder: What if we used an equation to transmit this information? I therefore added a multiplication sign between the word "Mi" and the numeral "2." I merged the "816" and "798." The equation then became: "Mi $\times$ 2 = 816, 798." Our core user groups all knew the significance of "816" and "798," the date and the place. The Mi 1 had been launched at the same time, same place, and one year earlier. Meanwhile, new and potential users would ask around to find out what the equation meant, and in doing so they would have even more of a sense of expectation.

"Leaving enough white space" means select, elite, cadence, and control in design. It shows that what you are conveying are core elements. You are implying a sense of emotion, or quality, while still leaving room for the imagination and allowing others to generate their own sense of expectation.

At the annual press conference in 2013, we used a "Sword Sabre" visual theme with certain ambiguities that made users wonder if we would be launching "weighty products" in two different product categories or launching a smartphone on two different platforms. The answer was that both of these were true.

The Mi router first began public trials at the end of 2013. In our initial Weibo ad campaign for this, we presented a photograph of one part of a frontal view of the product. Our Internet friends enthusiastically joined in guessing what the "second innovation" would be. The result was that the extraordinary power of group imagination generated a host of design proposals, such as "the first soybean milk machine for young people" and "a thermos bottle for rich people" (Figure 6.12).

年轻人的第一台豆浆机

全球首款Android系统智能豆浆机
高通骁龙600四核1.7G
2GB内存/8GB闪存
WiFi双频/蓝牙4.0
手机遥控 远程操作 颠覆性的交互方式
深度定制的MIUI V5豆浆版

FIGURE 6.12 *The Imagination of Soybean Milk Re-created from Mi Router by Mi Fans*

On May 15, 2014, we released an advance ad about a "viral campaign" that hinted that Xiaomi would be launching an entirely new product category—a kind of Mi pad—in its next product release.

One final example of using sufficient white space in your design: On April 23, 2014, we held a meeting to connect with social media representatives, prior to which we did warm-up publicity. Our primary text for this used the phrase "within the realm of emotions but outside the realm of expectations." The reason is that we were planning to release three new products: the Mi Router (Figure 6.13), Mi Router Mini, and Mi Box Plus. At the time, many people guessed that we would necessarily be launching a router and a box, but the mini-router was definitely outside the realm of expectations.

When we drew out the ad plans on a whiteboard, we first wrote the words, "April 23, within the realm of emotions but outside the realm of expectations" (Figure 6.14). After that came the words, "Xiaomi new product new product meeting to connect with social media." I saw that and said, "You've made a mistake," and the person at the whiteboard quickly crossed out one "new product." I immediately went over and instead wrote, "Xiaomi new product new product new product meeting to connect with social media." People started laughing as soon as they read this, and the result was that an enormous number of users clicked like when they later saw it on Weibo.

Ping 20.13.11.20 ▮

FIGURE 6.13 *The Poster of the Mi Router on Weibo*

The Only Standard by Which to Measure the Design Experience Is the Actual Location

At the end of the day, what is good design?

Like the price, product, promotion, and place (4P) theory in marketing, I sum up the design process as 3W + 1H: where, what, who, and how.

My phrase about designing with "hitting the nail on the head" in mind relates to "what" and "how." "Where," however, is a matter of the actual location. Is the design good design? You will only know once it gets to where it will be used (Figure 6.15).

FIGURE 6.14 *The Poster of the Press Conference on April 23*

FIGURE 6.15 *The Poster for the Press Conference on May 15*

We generally say that you have to be strategic in how you manage design. The best thing is not to change course for 10 years, to keep on target. Nevertheless, if your orientation is wrong to begin with, "keeping going" simply means you are being counterproductive.

How then do you determine that correct orientation? How do you avoid unmatching? The critical thing is to place the design in the required setting: Where is the design going to be used, and who is going to see it (Figure 6.16)?

FIGURE 6.16 *The only standard by which to measure the design experience is how it works in the actual location.*

The illustrations used in the above text were all designed in the midst of cracking a lot of jokes. They remind us that considerations about actual location are vital. Look at the example of Xiaomi itself. In May 2013, the GMIC Internet Convention was an extremely formidable occasion with 32 countries participating. We had to design a banner for the event, so we asked our most experienced designer to work on it, who then revised his own work multiple times and created five potential versions.

The one we decided on in the end looked as if it had not been designed at all (Figure 6.17). A glance at it made you think it was designed in some print shop or that it was being handed out as a free sample when you went in to an office store to make copies of something.

FIGURE 6.17 *The Poster for the GMIC Convention*

Feedback at the actual location, however, confirmed that this banner outperformed all the others. It was hung above the entrance to the convention where people rushed in and out, so a posterlike approach and eye-catching colors were necessary. Too much design was equivalent to too much information, which interfered with the message.

When we are designing ads that will be put on the Internet, we examine designs critically and ask the designers to simulate putting them on different websites, to judge the results. When we design large-scale ads for building interiors, we print up versions of identical size and put them for a week in the office or near elevators to see how people respond. Depending on the feel that is generated, we revise the design, the image, or even the size of the typeface to ensure that we get the best results.

Putting the ad in the actual location is the only standard by which you ultimately judge the effectiveness of the design.

A Picture Is Worth a Thousand Words

We are living in an age of images—if you use them expressively, you don't need words.

An e-commerce business that has no physical store means that its website is the equivalent of its store. Selling goods therefore first requires that you sell images (Figure 6.18).

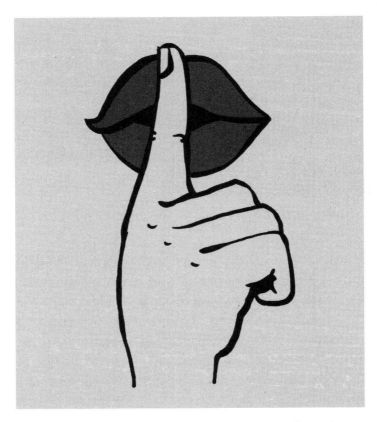

FIGURE 6.18 *A picture is worth a thousand words.*

Xiaomi deals only in premier goods, and it demands that all products be "explosive products." The company's website has been through three major revisions, and the way it displays images has been improved each time by emphasizing the key points. Put simply, that means the context for the images has become more and more simplified and "pure," while the images themselves have become larger. The latest website version has adopted a magazine format for displaying large images, and the quality is such that there is no need to write the name of the product as a selling point. The photos themselves attract users to click the image.

We use images to the utmost not only in e-commerce but also in transmitting our core events.

In 2014, we broadcast the entire Mi Fans Festival online. We transmitted the real-time digitized video of the event superimposed on images that had been prepared in advance. Once the day's activities were over, we also immediately produced a long blog message of images as the most direct way to enable people to perceive the event.

Users' attention span is extremely short in the age of mobile Internet. In an ocean of fragmented information, a fresh image trumps any number of words when it comes to making users pay attention or making them linger over your message.

Direct perception and intuitive understanding is the *attention dividend* that is most apparent in an age of images. One image is worth a thousand words. How, then, do you design that one image? There are many tricks that one can adopt. Without going into all the aesthetic considerations, I put a few of them below:

1. **Simple and straightforward.** Being simple is not the same as being rough. Instead, it means expressing the unique features of a product in the most appropriate way. The ideal situation is achieved when any more information in the image would be too much, while anything less would be incomplete. I often ask designers if they can possibly "get rid of this element," which is really a way of asking them to think about which elements are crucial and which are not.

2. **Feelings that can be understood intuitively.** One can express feelings without any words. For example, our case product is a soft green color. To set it off, our photographer put it in a setting of small props that gave it a warm and appealing look.

3. **Appropriate for viewing on mobile devices.** Each image should take a phone screen or a pad or notebook into consideration when considering what the user will experience. Our designers often use a 27-inch screen to display their work, which looks absolutely marvelous but which often does not reproduce on a phone. When considering the final results, I always ask designers to show it to me on a phone.

Images can express both form and color, while you have to actually read words and then interpret them. From the perspective of transmitting information, however, videos are even more effective than still images. One picture is worth a thousand words, but one video is worth a thousand pictures. Naturally, if you have great video material, you still need an initial image to draw in the audience (Figure 6.19).

Designers and software engineers are equally important in a mobile Internet company. Many things require fast response when they are being transmitted by social media. The in-house design team is of crucial importance in making sure images are passed along quickly and also with sufficient quality. In this age of images, if you have any idea that you want to start a company, you had better make sure you have an excellent designer on board from the very beginning.

When Interviewing Designers, Look, Ask, and Compare

I myself started out as a designer. Most founders of companies that I run into, however, have either technical or marketing backgrounds. Very few came out of the field of design. When they want to hire designers, they therefore ask me to recommend people, or they ask me how to interview people for the job (Figure 6.20).

Whether or not a designer is talented depends on whether that person is capable or pretentious. My method of interviewing people and finding this out is quite simple: look, ask, and compare.

"Look" means to see what he or she is wearing—that is, I judge the applicants by their appearance and whether or not they have style themselves.

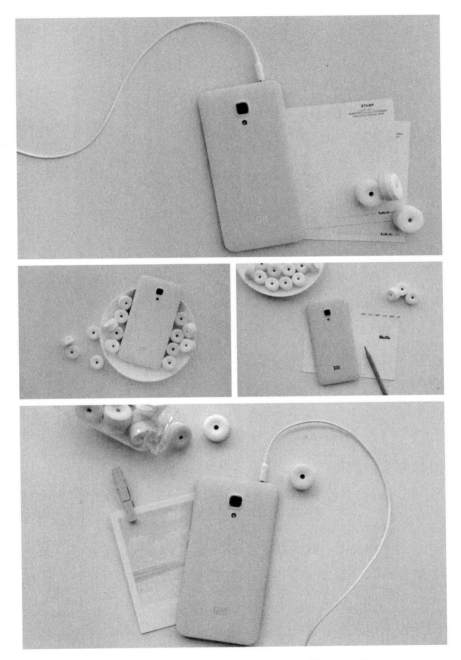

FIGURE 6.19 *The Design of the Phone Battery Cover*

FIGURE 6.20 *When interviewing designers, look, ask, and compare.*

Here "appearance" does not mean whether the lady is beautiful or the man is handsome on the outside. It refers to temperament and mental aura. Meanwhile, the "style" also is not a matter of long hair, trimmed beard, and so on. But seeing a person's clothes, shoes, and hat can indeed give you a sense of that person's aesthetic capabilities and ability to organize things. They can give you an intuitive sense of the person's character and quality of life.

"Ask" means to ask what they play with, what they read or watch.

In asking this, I get a sense of how much good design the applicants have seen, in their life and in their work.

In a certain sense, creating designs is a matter of redesigning and reorganizing all kinds of design elements. It is helpful to have seen a great deal of good design if one wants to be effective as a designer. At the same time, having good designers around you serves as frames of reference, as coordinates that help structure your own thinking. Sometimes they are what determine the mental horizon of designers.

When I am looking for designers for MIUI's interface, I generally ask people what apps they use on their phone. I even ask them to open up their phone to show me how many things they have inside.

If applicants do not have ongoing fresh stimulation in their own field of endeavor, if they do not stay enthused about their research or their play, I do not believe they can turn into outstanding designers.

Asking applicants what they read is mainly to see if they are in the habit of reading things deeply.

How do you make judgments about designers' field of perception? You can always ask them if they are in the habit of studying subjects in depth. Many designers are not—they enjoy looking at and finding material on the web. This superficial approach provides information, images, and design elements that can spark ideas and a certain feeling, but those ideas are fragmented and do not allow for any kind of systematic knowledge acquisition.

In my younger days, after creating a lot of projects on the front line, I spent a great deal of time rereading the design masters that I most loved and respected. I revisited their works and re-analyzed them along a vertical axis, which allowed for a systematic understanding of the ways of thinking that informed their designs.

The capable comes after you get through the pretentious. If you basically have the feeling that the applicants are not too bad, once you have looked and asked, then at least you'll know if the applicants are pretentious in their designs. The next step is the challenge of determining whether or not they are capable.

"Compare" means observing the detail in their works, seeing if their design style is consistent, and getting to know their attitude about designing.

Naturally, many rules don't apply when you are faced with good work and real designers, such as their mental aura or professional background. One more thing—when you are looking for a designer, you have to take success rate into account and make sure that the specific position is appropriate for the specific person. This is critical. Don't run around looking for an omnipotent superman. Distinguish between designers who have this or that talent—for example, those who are good at videos or those who are good at interactive designs, since the two are not the same and the demands that you place on that designer should not be the same.

Here Are Three Tips for Design Management

In order to ensure that messages are immediately and intuitively understood, the point is to "hit the nail on the head." This is the style of design that relies on an outstanding design team. However, the team must be managed effectively in order to maximize its capabilities. Here are three tips for design management: stick to the strategy, implement it to the end, and liberate your team (Figure 6.21).

FIGURE 6.21 *Three Tips for Design Management*

In designing a completely new product, you first have to consider the definition of the company itself—that is, the "who am I" question. What's more, you need to carry out a lot of fundamental work surrounding this question. The course of developing a brand is nothing more than a three-step process: popularity, reputation, and loyalty. "Popularity" means making sure people know who you are, making sure you are within their field of vision. "Reputation" means making sure people are willing to walk alongside by you, that you are okay. "Loyalty," in contrast, is making people really love you, making them want to internalize you and make you a part of themselves.

How do you start creating popularity for a brand? First, you have to spend time thinking things through very carefully—whether that is about the company name, or the appearance of the products, or the vision of the company. This fundamental work requires a great deal of energy and chewing things over time and again. Only once you have those things in mind can you begin to approach your products and your market in a systematic way. According to your own unique DNA, you then approach design in a fresh and unique way. Defining your strategy is hard, but sticking to that strategy as you implement it is even harder. During this time, you have to go through tremendous trials and make quite a few choices. A good strategy is one that you can stick to for 10 years without having to move off course.

Once you have a firm strategy, you look at how to implement it to the very end. How do you do that? You constantly revise things and change them. Change! Change! Change! And then? As long as you still have time, you keep on changing. And then? Change again!

Once we had defined the objectives of our strategic design and we had mustered the force to implement them to the end, the next key thing was to learn how to liberate our team. This was done to stimulate greater productivity and to provide organizational safeguards for design management. A central part of this involved getting employees to love their product. By that time we all had become decision-making managers; we had to learn transposition thinking and consideration for others.

Xiaomi was created by a group of fanciers, so there was no need to be concerned about getting anyone to love the product. As a company, however, Xiaomi needs to maintain that feeling of enthusiasm and go further in inspiring the same excitement in employees. That means setting up reasonable mechanisms that allow the energy of "loving products" to be translated effectively into design. This subject inevitably comes back to the Hai Di Lao Hot Pot, from whom we all have learned so much. We would like for employees to have the kind of spontaneous approach to customers that comes from inside, and Hai Di Lao Hot Pot was the first to have immense regard and concern for its own employees.

One can learn a great deal about how to start the process of resolving issues from internal employee complaints. One of the most common complaints is, "Our product manager and designer don't cooperate with one another, which lowers our efficiency." Behind this issue is something many companies have not truly become aware of—namely, that the speed at which Internet projects are developed has changed from being annual to being daily. Faced with this accelerated pace of changing generations of software, you have to set up auxiliary teams on projects. The most effective way to do this is to disassemble the whole process into its component parts.

Right now, Xiaomi has around a hundred different design teams. No longer are they all in one huge design center, under one comprehensive framework. They have long since been assigned to various projects—that is, to the groups handling those projects. Moreover, within an overall project-oriented structure, there are no complicated appointments. No one needs to worry about when he or she might be promoted to deputy manager, or manager, because these things no longer exist. Employees are part of a team working directly with a product manager and a designer, which allows for the flexibility and efficiency of a small group.

Quite a few people have already taken note of this trend in the industry. Under the same overall brand and design strategy, different products and app locations will naturally place different demands on design style, method of expression, and channels of transmission. This is a trend that people are now referring to as "greater concentration of elements for more dispersed expression." At the same time, the designers and the product managers are increasingly merged into a kind of composite identity. The small-group model is clearly more suited to all these changes. Another complaint one often hears these days is that, when project teams are put together, they discover that a particular designer may work to high standards but what he or she comes up with is flashy and without real substance. It doesn't hit the right note. The crux of this problem is that you cannot design if you do not understand the user. That is why we ask all employees in Xiaomi to surf the BBSs, go on Weibo, constantly interact with users, listen to what they are saying, and let them engage in your products, marketing, and design. This is the very foundation of the business model in Xiaomi.

Xiaomi internally tells people to forget about KPIs. We have no KPIs, we say. Behind this is the fact that user feedback and a swift response are what drive developers. For example, when we developed MIUI, the designer, the software engineer, and the entire group surfed BBSs constantly, and then, at the end of every week, we incorporated user opinions into the next version. Design was decided upon by everyone. It wasn't a matter of the boss's feeling good one day and then telling you your work looked good. Instead, we all depended on the "vote" of users themselves. It was their consensus on design that made the design good. The force behind this involved a cyclical interaction: if you were conscientious about how you treated users and respected their opinions, they in turn treated you well.

The main thing when it comes to liberating a team is creating a situation in which the members of the team can play, can truly love their own product, and can love the users of their product.

CHAPTER 7

ALEE'S NOTEBOOK

Subculture: A Required Course for Any Product Manager

How does one make products that are irresistible to young people?

This is a complex question because it touches on many aspects of the task, including the product, marketing, and servicing, among others. My belief is that you have to go where young people go—that is the first scene. You have to experience that environment, take its temperature so to speak, before you can pull together enough feelings about how to make a product. Subculture is the first scene among young people today, and it is a required course for any product manager (Figure 7.1).

FIGURE 7.1 *Subculture is a required course for any product manager.*

Go Where Young People Go in the First Scene

Why go there? Let's take an example. Baidu Top Search Terms can display the rank and trending of the key terms searched for among different age groups (Figure 7.2).

FIGURE 7.2 *Baidu Top Search Terms in April 2014*

If we choose the category of videos and look at search results, we find not only that different age groups search for different things but that the structure of their searches is different. Even though the categories may be the same, such as the films *Due West: Our Sex Journey* and *Lust, Caution*, the ranking of items within that category is strikingly different. More important, the ranking list reflects differences in the places in which different demographic categories consume things. Certain films always rank first among young people who have vigorous hormones, and they always watch them online. That way, they do not have to be controlled by the schedules of movie theaters. That is why *Tiny Times* is at the top of the list online. In contrast, thirty-something people search for movies that are currently being shown in movie theaters—they simply are accustomed to going to theaters to watch movies.

If you want to learn about the movie tastes of young people and you go to theaters to do the research, you will be out of luck. The lesson is that you have to find out where your targeted users "want to be." What is their preferred locale? Then you can begin to ask what kind of locale has the greatest viewing value, and where the interests are most obviously trending. The answer will indicate the interests as well as mode of expression of young people, and the answer will in fact be subculture communities. In the early days, such communities included MOP, Tieba, Interest Group on Douban, and so on. In the last few years, new modes of expression have become more diverse, and more directly intuitive, such as bullet curtain websites and rage comics.

B Station is a very popular bullet curtain website right now. The first time I saw the videos and the constantly changing commentary that was overlapped on them, I was stunned. Faced with text that was different every minute and every second, my first reaction was to think, "How can you see the video in the midst of all this?" My colleagues told me that it soon became addictive. I therefore forced myself to go on watching for 15 minutes. I still felt cross-eyed. After watching for half an hour, I suddenly felt a kind of mental shift and was able to keep on watching. I discovered that I could in fact separate the text from the images and watch them separately—if I wanted to watch the video, I could, and if I wanted to watch the commentary, I could. I invite everyone to try it. The feeling was reminiscent of when we were young and trying to see three-dimensional images in a flat two-dimensional surface. Instead of trying to focus the eyes, we had to let them unfocus a little, and suddenly our vision would become three dimensional. It was that kind of feeling.

Looked at in the simplest terms, the thing that the rage comics and bullet curtains have in common is that they are both spoofs. Adults might call these things the generation of after-1990s or after-2000s phenomena. Examined more carefully, however, one can discover that not everything is merely bullet curtain. Except for videos and cartoons, young people are also watching the history lecture presented by Yi Zhongtian with bullet curtain.

The bullet curtain video site in Japan has even worked its way into the practice of politics in Japan. Debates in the Diet are now directly broadcast, with different candidates for the different parties vigorously voicing their political views. The material is then also put on Niconico, which belongs to UGC in Japan, so that people's comments on politicians can be expressed and interpreted by everyone right away.

Bullet curtain itself is basically a kind of content, but it is not limited to being content. It also represents the way young people watch videos. I often think about how I used to play with my phone as well as my computer when I watched television with my parents some dozen years ago. My parents would frown on this, saying that I needed to be more focused. The same logic applies today. At the outset, we adults may well feel that bullet curtain is an aberration, but this is mainly a reflection of not understanding the behavior of young people.

In fact, online communities that collect subculture groups are not merely a source of content. They are also a force for supporting product mechanisms that then become systemic in nature.

The bullet curtain site provides a complete editing tool for bullet curtain. Inside this are a number of high-level functions that help you create bullet curtain results that are simply extraordinary. The key thing that ensures that bullet curtain will continue to exist is that it not only provides a means of expression but it also provides a complete product-chain platform. Rage comics are the same. They have corresponding formula-driven platforms and tools. In fact, the most iconic emotions in rage comics are prepared in advance—all you have to do is re-create them in a kind of secondary creation on top of the videos and images that you like. It is this kind of powerful and complete product platform that mobilizes, encourages, and supports a huge number of low-brow-culture group participants to undertake "re-creation." This also corresponds to a feature of post-modernist culture: it involves mass-market creation as well as consumption, and it involves the deconstruction and then reassembly of classic elements. What's more, in contrast to the content produced by professional content makers, which then goes through professional media to be distributed through various channels to the public in the traditional manner, this subculture method is able to provide content to a far greater audience of users. It enables access with much lower barriers to entry. It generates much greater enthusiasm, and it is becoming a flourishing ecosystem that could be called a re-creation ecosystem. To use an example that is more easily understood by engineers, the essence of software development communities is re-creation. The difference is that the influence many low-brow-culture communities have is far greater in the arena of mass-market consumption, while the barriers to entry and engagement are far lower.

All of this represents an advance. The first scenes provide a sense of transcending the immediate locale, and they also provide the tools for carrying out re-creation. Using these tools, the re-created works of young people can be launched with great ease due to lower barriers to entry. In the process, young people derive an extremely strong sense of satisfaction from participating. Young people are keenly interested in expressing their own unique qualities, while at the same time they want to find people who share the same interests. In the past, traditional media and the lack of tools were massively limiting factors for young people with ideas—they kept young people from getting in contact with as well as influencing groups of people. Now, thanks to mobile telecommunications services that are constantly being improved, and thanks to social media networks, including rage comics and bullet curtain sites that provide both the tools and systems, young people can not only find like-minded companions more easily but they also can also share their own ideas more easily.

Young people are coming together to form subculture groups with shared interests. If we truly want to understand their likes and their interests, therefore, we have to go to low-brow-culture scenes. We have to be where these young people want to be.

The Essence of Change Is Consumer Demand

As noted above, I believe that all of this represents an advance. The question then becomes, how was this advance generated, how did it come to be? Answers to this question, and causes for it, can be found in consumer opinions and consumer habits.

My feeling is that this represents a new offshoot of the whole concept of consumption. Looking back across the evolution of consumption, at the outset people consumed functions, then later they consumed brands, and still later they consumed experiences. In the past two years, I have been talking a lot about this experience type of consumption. When we in the older generation bought a telephone, ours was the classic kind of function-model of consumption. We wanted to make phone calls.

The suppliers at that time were Motorola and Ericsson. Later came the brand age.

What emerged from the husk of the previous era was Nokia, with its emphasis on "Connecting People." That was a crazy period, when health product companies could say proudly that they were pasting ads everywhere, even on pigpens, such as San Zhu. Many design companies at the time were doing corporate-image design that was simply imitative, even though they could make a million RMB from just the "concept." It was crazy. Later, however, the "consumer experience" became the catchword of the modern age. For example, smartphone companies set up extremely lavish, high-end experience stores, trying their best to give consumers the idea, "You are not just buying a brand. You are now part of an extremely fine and enjoyable experience."

Change never stops, however. As it surges onward, my sense is that we have already entered an age of participatory consumption. This time, however, the change represents an entire revolution in the way of thinking about consumption.

Inculcating a sense of engagement is the very soul of Xiaomi. We feel that the new way of thinking about the participatory consumption presents entirely new demands on a company and on users, based on their evaluation of how engaged they feel. From the very start of thinking about a product, its branding, and its coding, we therefore try to figure out how best to enable users to re-create in the easiest way, to participate in the best way. Then, we constantly improve upon our product based on the opinions of those users. In the process of participating, users themselves feel an ongoing sense of accomplishment, so that the chain of events creates a positively reinforcing cycle.

We can say with certainty that what the younger generation consumes is a sense of engagement. This generation not only says, "I see and feel your product," but it also says, "I need to get involved in it, and I want to grow together with your brand."

Xiaomi has its own methodology. We first made the MIUI system, and only later did we make the hardware to fit it, the smartphone. MIUI was the first project I worked on in Xiaomi, and we decided upon a basic course of action from the very beginning: we would create a product that operated through the Internet and that was constantly being improved upon by user engagement. We would not "shut the door and make a car by ourselves."

Before we made smartphone systems, all other companies had a cycle of releasing products on a three-month or half-year basis. When we started making MIUI, we instead asked ourselves if we couldn't put out a new version every week, change generations weekly. There were just six of us working on MIUI when we were just starting up the company, and for a long time the number of employees came to just a few dozen people. Our idea was to mobilize the forces of these people, however, and create a development team that was equivalent to a force of 100,000.

Looking back on it now, it seems very simple. We started operating in the most primitive way, through BBSs. Each week we would release the revised product to the BBSs. In the course of doing this, our product managers began to communicate with users. The people working with the BBSs were not purely product managers, however, since we asked everyone to surf the BBSs and interact with users. Each Friday the upgrade went out and, on the following Tuesday and Wednesday, users would submit their user experience reports. We learned from these reports what revisions would be needed the following week and which of our teams had to do a little better. Internally, we relied on the votes of users to tell us whose improvements were excellent and had satisfied users, so that we had that tiny bit of an incentive. It made us structure our internal process in ways that truly relied on user votes to drive the R&D process forward. Changes were not made at the suggestion of some boss. They also were not made at the request of some particularly stubborn engineer.

In addition, we had offline activities such as MIPOP events to which we invited all users. When we played games together, our development team would be right there on the spot. In 2013, we did a total of 19 official MIPOP events, but other fans held such things on their own, and there must have been more than 500 of them. On December 27, 2013, we held our first Annual MIPOP Gala at Beijing's National Convention Center. The chief purpose of this activity was to thank and reward our users. On that day, our users were stars.

Mainstream Culture Is Also Emerging from Subculture

Encouraging a sense of engagement is a new form of marketing to consumer demand that is based on interactive feelings and mutually shared values. Given that, let us look at an even bigger example. Nowadays, AKB48 is the hottest girl idol group in Japan, but the entire AKB Group is in fact composed of more than 200 devotees. The appearance of this group can be regarded as the classic example in recent years of the emergence and success of the participatory type of consumer demand. AKB48 has taken in virtually all the recording awards and entertainment prizes that Japan has to offer. For several years in a row, it has been among the top names of the total ranking of bestselling songs in Japan. It is a phenomenon that is known to every household in the country.

The success of AKB48 was born over the course of eight years. At first, the girls were just an underground idol group in the Akihabara area of Tokyo. However, they then came up with the unprecedented concept of idols "who would meet you face-to-face." This was quite different from the traditional role of idols who kept a lofty distance. AKB designed a whole series of ways in which fans could have close contact with them and ways in which they and fans could interact. They even thought of ways in which fans could have an influence on their business. For example, they organized a nationwide "hand-shaking" event—when fans bought an album, they would also receive a hand-shaking coupon that allowed them actually to shake the hands of people in the group. The hands of group members would sometimes be swollen by the end of the day. Their "general election" system was an even greater innovation. When fans bought a single-song CD, they got the right to cast a vote for whichever member they liked most. This then determined the ranking of the songs on the CD and the order of the names on that song.

The entire system came well packaged with a variety of activities, not just one simple kind of event. There were elections for excellence in other categories, a graduation system, and an underground theater for fans, as well as online television programming. Once I began to understand this phenomenon, I realized that the general manager behind the scenes, a man named Akimoto Yasushi, is in fact an extremely great product manager.

He made the entire election process into a systematized platform, into a factory that creates dreams. In the course of all this, the thing that most moves people is that they can be face-to-face with an idol—that is, fans can grow up together with the members of the group.

On the one hand, paying attention to subculture allows us to know more accurately what the likes and interests of young users are today. On the other hand, it also allows us to have a taste of mainstream culture in the future.

There is a time lapse in the way subculture develops and evolves. For example, it took AKB48 eight years of hard work before they became fully mainstream in Japan.

Rock and roll is another example of this time lapse. By the late 1970s, rock and roll had already become mainstream in Europe and the United States while in China it was still regarded as beyond the pale. Today, rock and roll has become a kind of energy that is broadly accepted in China—today's popular music in China has a lot of rock and roll elements to it that are used with a kind of intensity that far surpasses the classic hard rock of the 1980s. What happened in between? Actually, as they say, "Old men don't go bad. It's more that bad men get old." The people who used to listen to rock and roll in the old days are now those with the voice, the "right to speak." They have become society's mainstream. When it started out, rock and roll was lowbrow. The spirit behind it now moves more people and has become the acceptable norm.

Kevin Kelly, the author of the book *Out of Control: The New Biology of Machines, Social Systems, and the Economic World*, has said that revolutionary innovations often come from the perimeter, the edges of systems. Indeed, we discover that much of mainstream culture has in fact come from subculture. By the time today's young people grow up, the young people who so love rage comics and AKB48, we can only imagine what their mainstream culture will be like in 15 or 20 years.

If you want to make products that young people are passionate about, you have to go to the first scene, the place they most want to be. Today, subculture is that place. Young people do not simply want function, and they do not simply want a brand. They want to feel engaged. We should look forward to the mainstream culture of the future and realize that we will be internalizing it ourselves. Indeed we can start that process today.

Making Technology Livable

I would like to talk a little about the idea of "technology in daily life"—that is, making technology livable. It sounds a little like the opposite side of "life technicalization" we were hearing years ago. Back then, the trend in the consumer electronics industry was to want to embed technological elements into our lives, to emphasize the technological feel of things. Now, we have "technology in daily life"—but what does it mean? My understanding of it is that technology should have the power to comfort people and please them (Figure 7.3).

One could say that life technicalization meant dazzling us with technological wonders. In contrast, "technology in daily life" is more like enabling technology to make us happy.

FIGURE 7.3 *Technology should bring comfort to the human soul.*

Here is an example: 2012 was the first year that wearable devices really became "the thing." The forecast was that they would be coming onto the market rapidly by the year 2014. My take on the ones you actually see around today, however, is that they are primitive and just the very start of what they may be in the future.

If you look carefully, you'll notice that the promotion material on these wearable devices talks a lot about their fabulous technology, while the degree of detail put into the look of these things is minimal. The classic example of something wearable is jewelry. All jewelry is made with exquisite attention to detail and to beauty. If these devices are not as well crafted as jewelry, how can you expect anyone to wear them all day long? I wore a band myself for a while but got rid of it after a month or two.

If you want these devices to truly develop in the future, and if you expect users to want to wear them daily, you definitely need to put more thought into how comfortable and appealing their external design is, and you need to make changes.

The watershed in this whole arena came at the end of the twentieth century. Before that, the terminology that everyone used to describe the design of mass-consumer products exaggerated the technological aspects. People talked about lasers, complex human-machine interfaces, and so on. In contrast, at the end of the last century, the kind of thinking espoused by Apple began to emerge with a successful focus on the consumer. Starting from the time the iPod beat out products that had a more engineered and mechanistic feel to them, such as the MD and the Zen hard disk player, this wave became unstoppable. The iPod era represents youth, fashion, and freedom.

We can therefore understand the appearance of wearable devices such as bands, heart rate belts, and so on. Their functionality may involve simply measuring how many steps you take or recording changes in your weight, but their underlying essential attribute is something quite different: they allow you to understand yourself better. This then involves caring for yourself, looking after yourself. In the simplest terms, it is pleasing yourself. In fact, the sense of pleasure that such devices provide is not just a matter of initial interest. (Such interest in the products is widespread and usually from geeks.) Instead, the pleasure is similar to the feeling one might get from walking with a girlfriend down the street, looking over fashion magazines, or watching a romantic film—again, pleasing oneself.

The consumer electronics industry is now not simply technology stimulated. Instead, it is also "pushed" by consumers' emotion. It will not return to being a colorless high-tech industry. Instead, just like other consumer goods, fashion, high cuisine, and so on, it has to focus on design, and it has to focus on consumers' emotion.

In this age in which the combination of technology and design necessarily refer to "Apple," is there any other model worth evaluating, any more pure example?

In thinking about this whole idea of "technology into daily life," I would like to recommend a brand for your consideration: MUJI (Figure 7.4).

FIGURE 7.4 *The Poster for MUJI*

I have enormous respect for this brand. MUJI has been my inspiration for a long time. The feeling of elegance that its design imparts is truly comforting to the human heart.

The thing that first attracted me to MUJI was an ad shot back in 2003, which completely won me over. It was of the entire horizon at a lake in Bolivia that is known as the "mirror in the sky," the Uyuni Salt Lake. The sense of space draws you in and is completely relaxing. The MUJI team also went to Inner Mongolia to photograph a sunrise that similarly gives you a sense of the horizon—the aesthetic approach of the brand is ultra artistic.

The first product that attracted me to MUJI was a CD player that was designed by Naoto Fukasawa. He used the classic design of a wall-mounted fan. When you slide on the music switch, the sound comes out at you like currents of air from the fan (Figure 7.5).

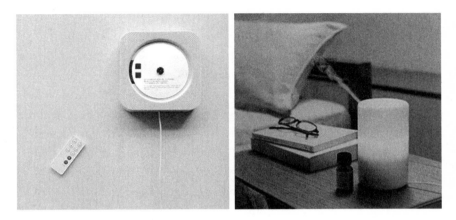

FIGURE 7.5 *The CD Player and Humidifier of MUJI*

Another example is the humidifier that is constantly here on my desk. It is designed in a way that makes it seem to be having a conversation with you—its rounded corners and polished-sand materials make you think of something soft and communicable. The design of the brightness of two lighted sections is perfect—when the soft light comes on, you suddenly feel warm and cozy.

MUJI comes from a lifestyle brand in Japan originally called Mu Jirushi Quality Products. The words *mu jirushi* can be translated as meaning products that carry no trademark, or no brand, but that still are outstanding in quality. From the beginning, the company has made items for daily use which, by now, encompass almost everything including tech-oriented electronics. The success of this brand has challenged all traditional theory about branding. Traditional brands live in fear of two things. The first is not having brand recognition. Not having a brand at all is simply peculiar—most companies stick their brands on everything possible, particularly when it comes to luxury goods. Not having a brand to promote is definitely untraditional. The second is a lack of focus. Brands generally try not to cover too much—many therefore make only electronics but not clothes, or they make clothes but not electronics. Instead, MUJI covers almost everything. What is the magical force behind this company? Many people would like to find this out.

MUJI was born in 1980. Post-war 1980s Japan had developed to a stage of "pursuing consumption excessively" in terms of design. Many products were over the top, with excessive use of decorative elements. MUJI instead began promoting products that were "good enough" for just using. It began designing for "need" and not for "desire," to design for "this is just right" and not "too much." While using the world's best designers and the best craftsmanship and manufacturing processes, the company also sold it products at reasonable prices. In this regard, it was like present-day Xiaomi—our power banks use world-class high-quality materials and craftsmanship, but we sell them at just RMB 69.

If you were to compare them, what is the difference between MUJI and Xiaomi? That is an interesting question. When MUJI was just starting out, its chief designer was a man named Tanaka Ikko, who became one of the world's great graphic designers. He defined MUJI from the very start in terms of three core elements. He said that in order to create a great brand, you needed good products, good information for use in promotion, and a good space or environment in which to display your products.

This was his keynote message from the beginning: not only must you have good products but you must publicize them in world-class media so that they will stand above the products and product advertising of others. Moreover, your publicizing should include superlative displays at the point of sale. MUJI put tremendous focus on the atmosphere of the selling venue, which the company felt should be like a home. Details of MUJI stores include taking out the ceiling so as to expose the pipes, placing handmade pots here and there, and even using signage that is as natural and handmade as possible. Staff members even used to go out to the countryside to find handmade baskets—this kind of traditional handicraft emphasized the natural qualities of an ideal home.

The unique characteristic of the MUJI company is felt when people walk into the MUJI store—they sense the beauty of the products, the elegance in how they are presented, and the serenity of the space itself. I personally feel that it is very worthwhile to study this further and, indeed, to do research on the MUJI brand.

Tanaka Ikko was the teacher of Hara Kenya, a man for whom I have even greater respect. The teacher defined the concept, but Hara Kenya took it a step further in making it great. As the most famous designer in Japan, he is also a university professor. He currently serves as the design director at MUJI as well as the art director.

The words "without" and "empty" are powerful design concepts at MUJI. That is, nothingness is also everything—which is how Hara Kenya defines it. Behind his design is an experimental way of thinking.

He once designed a graphic signage system for a maternity hospital in Japan, which I like very much (Figure 7.6). The signs giving directions in the hospital are wrapped in cotton—this is a maternity hospital, and in this context using fabric makes you think of softness, of warmth. It is not at all aggressive. Using fabric as a material posed challenges, however, since it can get dirty easily. Hara had considered that challenge already, however: if it gets dirty, you take it down and wash it. Customers will notice that it is still white and clean, and from this they will derive the sense that this hospital is reliable.

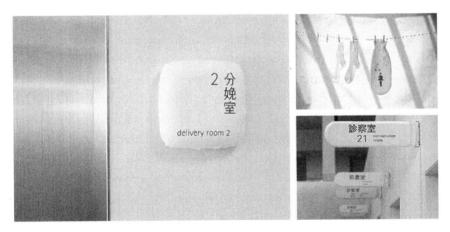

FIGURE 7.6 *A Graphic Signage System for a Maternity Hospital Designed by Hara Kenya*

What you begin to realize is that behind all good design is a way of thinking that reveals itself gradually: it imbues things with feelings, and it puts a kind of nurturing concern onto things. It instills in things a carefulness that is intuitively recognized. Industrial products that have no life to them whatsoever can be turned into signals for natural life and signals for feelings. This kind of design enables material things to have the kind of emotional appeal that makes people feel comforted and glad.

I believe that quite a few people in our age are waking up to the potential for a different kind of value, as they become "sick of loving things." Products with good design taste, the humidifier I mentioned earlier or Apple's MacBook series, give you a curative feeling simply by touching them. Things that show vigor, energy, gentleness, and elegance through their design, a range of emotions, are in themselves comforting to people.

The "fetishes" of consumers are constantly changing. In the world of design, this can be epitomized by the two different trends in product design—one toward a technical feeling and the other toward a made-for-actual-living feeling. If we look at how consumer electronics have developed in modern times, we find that there is an emphasis on technology for technology's sake at a certain period when economies are undergoing rapid development and societies are changing fast. The functions of electronic goods surpass the actual needs of their times and, in a sense, exaggerate the future. When the usefulness of Moore's law becomes less clear, however, and when the tide of consumerism recedes, user taste that was more inclined toward technical terms tends to become gentler and softer. It favors design that simply incorporates technology into products that are made for living itself.

Simply, the former trend loves the excitement and risk of exploring the future, while the latter is more internally focused and concentrates more on understanding oneself.

In the future, any brand that truly understands consumers' emotions must be one that has designers and artists behind it, in addition to a team of engineers. All of these people have a highly developed intuitive sense about life.

Finally, I would like to introduce two books that may be helpful in exploring what I have called the need for systematic study, specifically with regard to understanding the kind of design philosophy behind MUJI. One is called simply the *MUJI Book*, and the other, written by Hara Kenya, is called *Designing Design*.

Passion to Match the Creative Drive of Artists

Like creating anything, founding a company is a marathon and mostly done alone. There are the occasional applause and attention, but it is generally a solitary endeavor. This applies as much to the first step as to the ultimate ending. What supports you throughout, gritting your teeth as you endure, is nothing more than passion. Nothing else can stay the course (Figure 7.7).

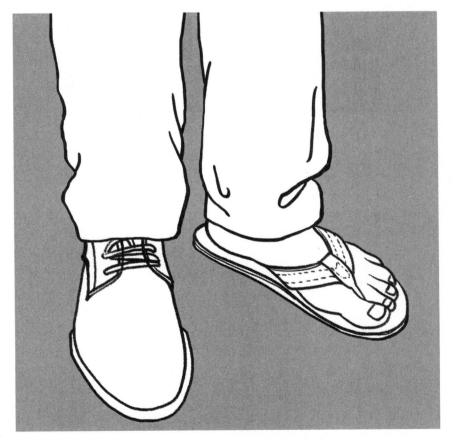

FIGURE 7.7 *Passion has to match the creative drive of artists.*

Everyone is well aware that start-ups are tough. All those who are engaged in the process confirm as well that their passion is not only inevitable but necessary.

In February 2014, the team in mi.com moved into the new office at Qinghe (Figure 7.8). This was several hundred meters away from the company's headquarters.

FIGURE 7.8 *First View of the Office in Qinghe*

Our younger colleagues then decorated the new space to look like an open art gallery for paintings (Figure 7.9). They hung paintings by famous names from art history and design history in all the rooms, and then they named the conference halls after artists, Chinese and foreign, historical as well as modern. Rembrandt, Yayoi Kusama, Vincent Willem van Gogh, Wu Guanzhong, and Zhu Da were included.

I am a designer by training, and I enjoy reading about art. Looking through illustrated books by various artists that I generally have on hand, I have been struck by the stories and emotions that have emerged from these people's lives that have transcended their own individual situations. As these young people were hanging the paintings, therefore, I realized they were not simply making their office environment more elegant and comfortable. They also were not trying to civilize employees by immersing them in art. The most important thing they were surrounding themselves with was something they could sense as a group—namely, the passion

FIGURE 7.9 *Second View of the Xiaomi Office*

that was embodied in these timeless works of art. This was something that preserved and protected the ideals for which these young people were striving and that upheld the desire for excellence and beauty in all they did.

A reporter once asked me what my hopes were for the future. My answer: I hope to keep the passion.

I would like to share with you some of the ways in which I have come to understand this word *passion*. The best way is to look at some of those stories of the masters that I mentioned:

- **Auguste Rodin, *The Gates of Hell*.** Auguste Rodin is renowned as the first great realistic sculptor of the nineteenth and early twentieth centuries. His most famous work, *The Thinker*, was originally intended to be placed on the upper part of the unfinished *The Gates of Hell*. This work was to have a total of 186 sculpted images according to Rodin's conception. Rodin worked on this for 37 years, continuing to revise it until the year before he died, and it is hard to imagine what sustained him over this long period if it was not passion.
- **Claude Monet, *The Water-Lily Pond*.** As one of the founders of the impressionist school of painting, Claude Monet had become internationally famous by around 1920, and he had earned enough money to establish a large studio. His paintings were being collected for the national collection, yet Monet suffered from cataracts on his eyes. In 1923, he had two operations, but his vision continued to deteriorate. Despite this, he continued to paint. In later years, he enjoyed sitting beside his small lake to paint water lilies, and then he carried on with painting these as his primary subject, making the canvases ever larger as time went on. He was nearly blind at the end, yet he continued to paint until his death on December 5, 1926. When I first saw some of these paintings at the Orange County Museum of Art, the surface of the painting seemed to pass through both time and space as the story behind the image came to mind, and emotions welled up inside.
- **Pierre-Auguste Renoir, keeping his dream while in a wheelchair.** Another important member of the impressionist school of painting, Pierre-Auguste Renoir was famous for painting people with rounded faces and hands and smiling countenances. He excelled at depicting

sunny emotions—rarely do you find any pain or hardship in his works, or anything to do with religion. Instead, you often feel the warmth of motherhood or sisterly affection. Nevertheless, in around 1892, Renoir began to be afflicted with rheumatoid arthritis, which greatly limited his activities for the last 20 years of his life. Forced to work from a wheelchair, Renoir would rely on an assistant to place the brush in his hand in order to be able to continue to paint.

- **Wu Guanzhong, pursuing excellence.** Wu Guanzhong is a famous contemporary Chinese painter. As early as 1989, his paintings were being auctioned for record prices for a living Chinese painter—*The Ruins of Gaochang* sold for 1.87 million Hong Kong dollars in that year. In 2007, his work *Ancient City of Jiaohe* sold for a new record for a contemporary Chinese artist at the time, RMB 4.07 million. His paintings are invaluable, yet the painter himself lives a simple life in an older residential neighborhood in Beijing's Fangzhuang area. When he and his wife go out for a stroll, few people around realize that this is a famous painter whose paintings sell for millions. In September 1991, Wu Guanzhong went through his paintings and selected several hundred that he personally felt were not up to his own standards. He then put them to the torch. Since his paintings were already priceless at the time, people have referred to this action as "burning down the house."

There are plenty of other stories that could be told, strange and wonderful things about artists, but the thing that I find most extraordinary in them is the purity and the passion that they have toward their endeavor. A person's success in any endeavor is inseparable from this kind of passion.

Looking at the subject from a different perspective, as long as any of us holds onto a kind of passion about what we are doing, we will be willing to keep learning about it, immerse ourselves in it, do it with all we've got.

Our passion comes from self-realization. It has to do with our hopes, our sense of accomplishment, and our sense of glory as well, but it also has to do with internal reflection. One such mode of reflection comes from the simple, pure appreciation of great works of art. This is perhaps the greatest incentive of all, driving us on to excellence. Through a self-impelled, self-driven process, it allows us to return to the origin and forget gain and loss.

Lessons Derived from Photographic Equipment

Xiaomi sells through word-of-mouth reputation. I am a designer and not a marketing person, but many years of playing with photographic equipment have taught me things about retail marketing.

As a photography fancier, I could more accurately be described as a spendthrift.

The greatest crime in this regard is that, as they say, "if you are a photography fancier, your descendants are poor." Nevertheless, I comfort myself with the thought that I have cultivated my own sensitivities and derived great pleasure from the process. I often tell friends whom I am trying to cultivate in a similar fashion, "Interest can be your psychologist." That is why it has been necessary for me to have that camera I like so much (Figure 7.10).

I bought my first camera more than 20 years ago, probably around 1991. It was a Ricoh XR8, and it used film. The person who advised me to buy it was my buddy Ziqian from my class in middle school. At that time, he was the head of the school's photography association.

I bought my second camera in 2000, when I had just begun work. It was a Nikon F80, also known as the poor man's F100. It had a Tamron 28- to 105-millimeter lens. The one who recommended this camera to me was the little brother of a classmate from high school. The older brother's name was Zewen, and the younger brother's name was Jingwen. Jingwen went on to be a professional photographer—a photojournalist for a well-known news agency.

My third camera came when I had just moved to Beijing. It was a Canon S70, which was a card digital camera. I went online to surf BBSs to research it. At that time, the digital single-lens reflex was still extremely expensive. The thing that impressed me about the S70 was the price point of 3,000—it was a digital camera, but it was still affordable.

The fourth camera I bought, in 2006, was a Canon 5D. At the time, this was the classic digital camera for the common man. At that time,

FIGURE 7.10 *Lessons Derived from Photographic Equipment*

I was spending all day surfing BBSs to choose the body, lens, and other parameters of the camera. I made up my mind only after nearly three months of searching on BBSs.

After that, I played with quite a few more cameras, including full-frame digital SLR, Leica M8, Sigma DP1, and Sony NEX7, and I had enough lenses to cover the top of a large table. Right now, the ones I use most are a Fuji XPro1, a Canon 5DIII, and a Leica S.

In chatting about photography with a journalist friend, our conversation naturally gravitated to equipment and the idea of buying things on the basis of friends' recommendations. She suddenly said, "There are not many Mi Fans at all. Since Xiaomi regards itself as being born for fans, what are you going to do when you have more and more users? How are you going to handle more of a mass market?"

This was a marvelous question.

What is it that real fanciers focus on? In a few words, you could say, "unique and sophisticated." If a product is taken to the ultimate excellence in any given regard, fanciers will naturally go for it.

Leica is an example. People used to say that Leica was not keeping up with the times. Nevertheless, the elegance of its cameras and its tastefulness still put Leica at the apex of professional brands. Or you can talk about the Sigma DP system—many people discuss its many weaknesses, and indeed it does have a problem with slow focus, but its three-tiered CCD technology gives its photographs the quality of a painting. It has a large-sized sensor that approaches the level of the APS-C digital single-lens reflex. As a small-sized digital camera, it is still quite admirable.

All of this also explains why Mi has aimed for high functionality from the beginning. As long as the functionality is outstanding and the character is clear, there will definitely be people who want it.

The ones who appreciate your product first are the core potential users. These are the opinion leaders among fancier groups. What's more, in the business of consumer electronics, the critical evaluations of opinion leaders have a major influence on purchasing decisions.

At the very beginning, I bought my Ricon camera and Nikon digital single-lens reflex with film based on the recommendations of friends who were familiar with that line of business (Figure 7.11). Later, as I felt my way forward, I began to use my own judgment to decide what I liked. At that point, however, the character of the brand became more important to me—indeed, it had the greatest influence. For a full-frame, digital single-lens reflex camera, for example, I chose the Canon. Even though Nikon had a sharper image overall and stronger contrast, I liked the red circle on the Canon lens over the gold circle on the Nikon lens. What's more, the Canon image quality was softer, and it had a greater depth.

FIGURE 7.11 *Photos by Alee*

Opinion leaders among fanciers provide the power of the word-of-mouth marketing, which is now multiplied countless times by the emergence of social media. Before, fanciers were a limited market in themselves, and the number of people they could influence was limited to their circle of immediate friends, acquaintances, and family members around them. Now, you do not need to make a phone call or get on professional BBSs to get advice—it is extremely easy to get recommendations from microblogs and WeChat.

The pathways we now take in order to reach consumers are therefore much shorter and also much flatter.

Because of this, marketing can achieve unprecedented success when products are conceived in ways that cement the relationship with fanciers. What's more, the kind of products that Xiaomi wants to make, like phones and TVs, are classic standardized mass-market items. We aim to be the national brand in these things and to be popularized in social media.

We therefore can respond with a certain degree of confidence to the marvelous question I have been asked: "In today's market, once you mobilize fanciers, how can you mobilize the market itself?" What fanciers like are consumer electronics that represent excellent taste.

I would like to thank my journalist friend for reminding me, as we chatted, of the subconscious source of the rhythm by which Xiaomi spreads word about its products. Xiaomi positions itself as "being born for fans." In fact, at the beginning it was born for eight founders who were simply advocates of playing in a certain way. Its so-called marketing was a matter of sharing with others the kind of playing and sharing experiences that we had ourselves enjoyed.

Earlier, I mentioned the topic of "the pathway to growing a brand." This is in fact marked by the rhythm of how the brand is first near the users, then beside them, and finally internalized within them.

In contrast, the great majority of traditional brands follow the sequential path: popularity to reputation to loyalty. That requires putting enormous amounts of investment into the enterprise at the outset, investing in ads as much as you can. For better or for worse, let the user know the brand first. Later you can broadcast the quality of the products. Certain products, such as melatonin, in China's healthcare industry, are a classic example of this type of product launch.

For Internet-based companies, however, the sequential path is this: reputation to popularity to loyalty. An Internet business is part of the experience economy, and its product is the experience and also the brand. Once the thing is experienced, it can be rapidly broadcast throughout the Internet. It's like using a search engine. You usually do not choose a particular one because you have seen an ad for that search engine. You choose it because your friends are using it. It is very hard, however, to generate loyalty on a traditional Internet platform. Whether a user stays with you or goes elsewhere is determined by the value of a particular tool. The classic example is watching videos on the Internet. With so many sites to choose from, you go to wherever there is something worthwhile to see. The pathway is then basically shortened to reputation to popularity.

What about Xiaomi? Our rhythm is a little different.

The pathway to growing a brand for Xiaomi has been reputation to loyalty to popularity.

Like other Internet-based companies, we too first focused on making our products have a good reputation. We wanted users to know that the products were good. The next step, however, was not to worry too much about popularity. Instead, we cultivated the first wave of loyalty from users who approved of our product. In the online community, we consciously sought to tie in core users and to win over a great number of Mi Fans. Only in 2013, three years after the company was founded, did we begin to experiment with advertising. Only then did we start to expand our popularity. By that time, we had already generated sufficient potential energy in our brand by amassing fanciers who approved of us and Mi Fans who were loyal to us. Once we had already achieved a critical mass of fans, spending on promotion could be more effective.

Finally, the last question my journalist friend asked me was, "What hopes do you have for the future?"

My answer was, "I hope to keep the passion."

She said, "Can you be more specific?"

I said, "When things quiet down, I would like to create paintings of some of the photographs I have taken."

I continue to believe that what will carry on through time is not commerce but rather philosophy, literature, and art.

Internet Transformation of Company Needs: "Explosive, Flat, and Gladness"

If you don't keep transforming yourself, are you just waiting to die? And if you transform, are you killing yourself in the process?

In the second half of 2014, we were talking things over with a number of entrepreneurs in traditional industries, and we discovered that many of them were anxious. The previous year, everyone had been talking about Internet thinking, but it seemed that this year everyone was afflicted with Internet anxiety disorder. Everyone was asking if we had any good ideas about transforming their Internet models.

Everybody thinks that Xiaomi has used a number of clever tricks in Internet transformation. For example, since Xiaomi uses only Weibo and other social media, these people also then stopped putting money into advertising—and they were astonished when Xiaomi started advertising on CCTV. Many of these traditional companies view Internet transformation as a kind of surgical operation. They will perform the operation wherever it hurts, and even amputate directly. I myself think this is the wrong way to go about things.

Instead of major principles, however, I can only offer one thing: Internet transformation needs to be internal and external. In this regard, I call it "explosive, flat, and gladness" (Figure 7.12).

FIGURE 7.12 *Internet Transformation of Company Needs: "Explosive, Flat, and Gladness"*

The core concept here follows three lines of thinking.

The first is "explosive." Product tactics and product structure have to be explosive. There is no way you can maintain interactivity with users on several hundred product lines. Nobody has that kind of energy. A few days ago, I met with the head of a traditional home appliances company that has been in business for close to 30 years. He said, "I like your idea, but we already have several hundred kinds of products. Users have opinions on all of them—how do we sift through them all?"

I responded, "Why do you want several hundred products?"

The rationale for explosive products represents the most fundamental and simple logic behind Xiaomi. If we did not make our products explosive, we would not be able to make users crazy or enable them to have a sense of engagement. Explosive does not just mean making superlative products. Everybody wants to make premier products, but most of the time they also want to make a dozen of them. That's wrong. Can you make only one? Can you make only two? Making one or two explosive products is enough.

The second is "flat." Organizational structure should be combed through and flattened. Companies in the Internet age must be able to motivate people and generate innovative behavior if they intend to take the path of reaching the public at large. To do that, you have to flatten. How can there be any creativity at all if you have multiple tiers in your organizational structure with each level reporting up to the next? If you have five or six levels, maybe even seven or eight, it takes the company two or three months to make a decision.

Let's say you are an engineer with an idea. Since you yourself don't count, you make a proposal, and it goes through seven or eight levels of bosses before an opinion gets back to you. No engineer is going to have the courage to face that and still be innovative. In Xiaomi, many of our users know exactly which software engineer created which function, which piece of programming was done by which engineer. When someone rejects something, an engineer can say, "I noticed the feedback on this problem," and he can immediately get it fixed. The R&D in Xiaomi is basically structured in three levels. The first is the employees, the second is the core management team, and the third is the partners. Our R&D

departments in particular do not have overly complicated organizational structures, with managers, deputy managers, and so on.

When we carry out a complete transformation in Internet transformation, we definitely make it from inside to outside. We first build our organizational structure and our product structure to create an explosive product; then after that, we flatten out our organizational structure.

The third is "gladness." The thing that motivates a team is to make employees be glad. If you can make your employees be glad, there are no rules. For example, the way of doing things in Xiaomi may be appropriate for you, but it also may not. The most fundamental thing is for management to take employees' advice. Management has to be in the same place as employees, listening to what employees are thinking, how they can feel more participatory, and how they can get a greater sense of accomplishment. Are the incentives sufficient for them? All of this relates to straightforward, frank, and clear communication. Once employees feel glad, they ignite themselves.

When we select people to be on teams in Xiaomi, we require that they have both professional expertise and an entrepreneurial spirit. What's more, we provide team members with excellent compensation and excellent benefits. Not only do we give people money, however, but we also push them onto the front of the stage. When they provide service to customers, it helps a lot if they are the star of the team.

These things are what I mean by "explosive, flat, and gladness." When a boss is trying to make choices, he or she should be asking, "How am I going to cut a hundred product lines down to one?" "How am I going to get rid of all these apron strings?" "How can I reduce the unnecessary governance structure for political struggle?" As for employees, when there is a clear product structure in the company and a good organizational structure that truly respects them, they will naturally respond by being innovative. What's more, they will deliver good service. The most fundamental thing behind all of this is respect for human nature. Only if you respect your employees will they in turn respect customers. The logic is extremely simple. It is a great deal easier to comb through these things internally than it is to sit around and debate the right way to approach the Internet thinking.

With respect to the Internet as a whole, I believe we are living through an explosive and flat era. What does that mean for the harsh realities of the future? In the past, many industries could accommodate 10 or even 20 brands, given the asymmetry of information dissemination. The Internet revolution is an information revolution, however, which means that once information becomes symmetrical, the equation changes. Brands will become highly consolidated—each product category will allow for the existence of 3 to 5 brands. We know that the basic product categories of the Internet at present are search, security, and videos. Each of these has at most 5 brands, of which only 3 can be regarded as doing very well.

Behind explosive, flat, and gladness is the process of transforming a results-driven business into a creativity-driven business. This means understanding that the most outstanding people will put their greatest efforts and creativity into matters about which they are passionate.

In doing this, the first step is to remove KPIs. Not having KPIs does not imply, however, that the company does away with all targets and goals. How does Xiaomi separate out and allocate these goals? We do not force them onto employees. Instead, they are the responsibility of the partners. When we talk about the KPIs we have decided upon, moreover, we do it in overall quantified levels. For example, we might say that we intend to sell 40 million sets this year, but we do not make a deal with people and say, "If you sell at A level, B level, or C level, we will reward you with this or that." Meanwhile, if our sales team has a goal of 40 million but then suddenly sells 50 million, do we take a pot of money and spread it around, saying, "Go take a holiday in the Maldives"? No, we do not. That is not how we handle things. When we are determining KPIs, we're mainly making a judgment about where the company is on the staircase in terms of growth. After we have estimated that information with some degree of accuracy, we then can allocate the appropriate resources.

Compared to results, we are more concerned about process. As long as employees nail the process, the results come naturally.

Lei Jun's most profound saying is a phrase by Wang Yangming: "The humans' desire is the rules." The question of how to make employees glad is something any company can figure out, if the company takes the time and makes the effort to do so. When Lei Jun founded Xiaomi, he did it with a very open attitude and in a calm frame of mind. He had already built up companies for 20 years. He had long since established his reputation and made his contribution—he had both fame and money. Prior to working on Xiaomi, he had also been one of the most famous angel investors in China, so he certainly did not lack fame or money. Whether people believe it or not, he was dream driven to work on Xiaomi. That is, he wanted to create a company that was great "enough" and do something that was great "enough." Because of this, he provided his partners and our core employees with "enough" guarantees in the form of benefits, authority to proceed, and respect.

I have watched the way many companies tell their partners that they will provide them with employee stock options, but only when the companies are about to be listed on the stock exchange do they tell those partners exactly how many options. In contrast, Lei Jun has always laid things out clearly with the partners and with any core employees as soon as he has entered the company. With competition for talent the way it is today, you cannot simply talk about brotherly feelings. Without enough material incentives, that would make things tough.

Anyone who is a boss has to be responsible for constructing the entire team. Meanwhile, the partners in Xiaomi today have their own business, which they handle by themselves. If there is nothing going on that everyone needs to know about, basically each one does his or her own thing. Nobody interferes with anybody else. That means that each one can decide on his or her own the way things should be, which guarantees that decisions can be made very, very fast.

Hiring employees is handled the same way. Our method is to find the best people. To me, research and development has always been a highly creative activity—it is hard to do if you are not sufficiently intelligent but also if you are unable to relax. In finding the best people, one has to realize that a good engineer is someone who can go up against not just 10 others but 100 others. In terms of core engineers, therefore, none of us skimps on spending real capital. We certainly do not just sit back and hope that colleges will train the talent for us. The best people have a kind of driving force within themselves—all you have to do is put them in the right position, allow them to have a frame of mind in which they can "play," and they will truly perform.

What's more, only if they do mobilize their own performance will they then have the ability to inspire others. A lot of our engineers seem to be playing as they are being innovative. In hiring people, you therefore must find out what they are good at doing, and what they enjoy doing, and then just let them do it. Overly strict controls on the R&D staff are counterproductive. Not only are engineers annoyed by rules and regulations but they also even dislike doing reports. Their attitude is, "Leave me alone." The users will manage them. When they make a good product, users will praise them. When they make a bad product and are criticized by users, they themselves will take the initiative to change it right away.

Explosive, flat, and gladness. As one joke has it, this means exploding the boss till he is flat and the employees are glad. "Flat" refers of course to flattening the structure of a company and reducing KPIs, but this is done under two very important conditions. The first is that the company has a first-rate team. The second is that the company's growth rate is fast enough. Speed is a form of management. Meanwhile, if a company is to grow at speed, its products must be explosive. Gladness is the key to forming a first-rate team.

I am immersed in the summer song of cicadas. The air-conditioning in my study is broken, and the open window finally lets in a cool breeze, toward evening. The tree outside the window seems dappled and blurred through the soft waving of the curtain.

The song of cicadas has stopped insensibly, and I feel more and more peaceful when I am writing.

My mind returns to the study in our old home in Maoming. There is a tree outside too. Nearly finished with this book now, I have the same feeling I had then—I had graduated from high school, and I was excited but apprehensive.

I started to write this book in early 2014, so it has taken nearly half a year. It has gone through three in-house evaluations, and close to 50 colleagues and friends have participated in helping me assemble materials and proofread the results. The first version came to more than 400 pages, but it has been edited down considerably in this third version, which is less than 300 pages.

Each time a version was evaluated in-house, young colleagues would provide me with moving case studies. I was tempted to give the work up many times due to my workload, but this kind of feedback always re-energized me. I would again take up the brush and keep on going. I thank these young people. They are the benefactors of my dreams.

Thank you to Lei Jun for encouraging me to write this book and giving me extremely helpful suggestions on the structure and overall approach. Through 10 years together at Kingsoft and another 4 in Xiaomi, Lei Jun has continued to be a teacher to me and also my wonderful friend. From him, I learned "keeping on target" and "generation." "Keeping on target" meant everything would be the ultimate excellence, while "generation" meant holding on to an attitude of constantly wanting to learn.

I remember when I had just returned to Beijing from Zhuhai in 2004, and it was 10 p.m. in the evening. Late as it was, after finishing up in the office, Lei Jun took me out to visit the heads of quite a few grassroots websites, to learn how to optimize our search engine and improve the operations of our website alliance, as well as how to gain the greatest amount of traffic for the least amount of cost. We once spent half a year totally immersed in registering domain names. He would often call in the middle of the night to say he had just won a superb domain name at auction, such as duowan.com and duokan.com.

I thank the alliance of the cofounders of Xiaomi and the colleagues in the company who worked with me on both MIUI and mi.com. We were highly fortunate to come together to create such an appealing company. When we were just setting up the first office, we went to a furniture factory on the outskirts of the city to buy tables and chairs, in order to save money. On the first day of work at this office, April 6, 2010, my dad began making millet porridge for us at 5 a.m. in the morning. It was hot and steaming when he brought it to us. The 14 of us at that time, the first team, cheered with bowls of millet porridge to one another. In that moment, I truly did feel that we were starting a revolution. Because of that feeling, we have kept the tradition of eating millet porridge every time we move into a new office.

Our first step was simply to make a smartphone that we ourselves liked. We had no idea that we would have over 60 million global users so quickly or that Xiaomi would now have nearly 6,000 employees. These four years have been like the journey of a dream, like a miraculous voyage.

I thank my wife and my family. They sacrificed many weekends and holidays that we might have spent together as I wrote this book—I thank them for their support and companionship, and I thank them for both the freedom and the love that they gave me throughout.

I am a designer, so I look at things from the perspective of product design. When it comes to marketing, my views are fairly unsystematic, and the cases I have described in this book are also just fragments of a bigger picture. The truth of the matter is that we were not very theoretical in our approach to things—either in our thinking or how we proceeded.

The best way to look at it is to realize that Xiaomi itself is a real-life case study.

In the 14 years that I have worked professionally, I have been a designer, a product manager, and a marketing and sales person, as well as a professional manager and now an entrepreneur. I was very lucky to hit this experience during two great commercial waves, first the Internet itself and then mobile Internet. We are all bubbles on a great wave—all the phenomena in the world happen in the context of that greater reality. What you have to do is simply keep going.

As the times change, and as the concept of consumption evolves, marketing methods and channels also evolve. Methods of handling each channel also morph into new methods. It is easy for us to recognize this superficially, but it is also easy to see only the surface of what is changing. When one quiets down, one begins to hear the deeper rumblings under the raging torrent. What is the origin of the unchanging things behind the changes?

I believe that each product, each new creation, is an embodiment of life.

Friedrich Wilhelm Nietzsche posed three questions: Who am I? Where did I come from? Where am I going?

Who am I? This is a matter of choosing the product—which means being clear in our own minds about what values we want our products to create.

Where did I come from? This is a matter of choosing the team. Products are created by teams—this is no longer the age of the individual hero. We must do everything possible to organize a good team.

Where am I going? This is chosen by users. Who is this product being designed for? The answer is that the product must first be designed for oneself.

In the process of creating products and starting a business, we first have to answer those questions.

What attitude do we bring to our own lives and endeavors?

In 1996, R. Kelly wrote a song for Michael Jordan named "I Believe I Can Fly." It is about dreams, hopes, and holding on.

"If I just believe it, there's nothing to it. I believe I can fly, I believe I can touch the sky."

I in turn wish the attitude that lies behind this song could touch every young person setting out on the path of his or her own creations, his or her own endeavors.

At the end of every journey is a new beginning.

Li Wanqiang

EVENTS

2010

- April 6: Xiaomi is set up.
- August 16: MIUI beta version is released.
- December 10: MiTalk beta version with Android system is released.
- December 20: The A round of financing is declared complete; the estimated value of the company is USD 250 million.

2011

- July 12: Xiaomi declares it is going into the smartphone market.
- August 16: The Mi is released, and the annual MIPOP Festival is held, both at the Dashanzi Art District; the Mi with 1.5 G memory and dual-core CPU is released; the number of MIUI users surpasses 500,000.
- September 5: Mi.com goes online; 300,000 advance orders come in within 34 hours when Mi is launched for the first time.
- December 20: The B round of financing is declared complete; the estimated value of the company is USD 1 billion.

2012

- April 6: The first annual Mi Fans Festival is held; the second anniversary of the company's founding.
- June 23: The C round of financing is declared complete; the estimated value of the company is USD 4 billion.

- August 16: The Mi 2 is released, with 1.5 G memory and a quad-core CPU.
- November 14: The Mi Box Plus is released.
- December 21: Xiaomi allies with Weibo to create the first batch of online purchasing through social media in China; 50,000 Mi 2 are sold within two minutes and five seconds, which becomes a milestone event in social media purchasing.
- December 31: 7.19 million phones are sold this year; the pre-tax operating revenue is RMB 12.65 billion.

2013

- April 9: Second Annual Mi Fans Festival; Mi 2S and Mi 2A are released; the company announces it is going into the markets of Chinese Taipei and Hong Kong (China) as the start of its international strategy.
- July 16: 7.03 million phones are sold; pre-tax operating revenues come to RMB 13.27 billion in the first half of 2013; the number of MIUI users surpasses 20 million.
- July 31: Redmi with TD system is released.
- August 12: 100,000 Redmi are sold on Qzone within 90 seconds; a new record is set when 7.45 million users place advance orders via web-based social media.
- August 22: The D round of financing is declared complete; the estimated value of the company comes to USD 10 billion.
- September 5: The product-release press conference for 2013 is held at the National Convention Center using a "Sword Sabre" theme; the Mi 3 and Mi TV are released.
- December 12: Lei Jun, CEO and chairman of Xiaomi, is chosen as China Economic Person of the Year for 2013.
- December 19: The Mi Router begins its first round of testing.

2014

- January 2: 18 million phones are sold; pre-tax operating revenues come to RMB 31.6 billion in 2013.
- February 11: Xiaomi is selected as one of the Global Top Fifty "most innovative companies" by the American magazine *Fast Company*.
- March 26: Redmi Note is released on Qzone; the advance orders reach 15 million, setting a new record.
- April 8: The Third Annual Mi Fans Festival is held; the fourth anniversary of the company's founding; 1.3 million Mi and Redmi are sold within 12 hours; total payments break through RMB 1.5 billion.
- April 22: Xiaomi announces it has begun using the global domain www.mi.com.
- April 23: The Mi TV 2 is released, as well as the Mi Router Mini and the Mi Box Plus with 4 K technology.
- May 15: The Mi TV 2 is released as well as the Mi pad; on the same day, Xiaomi announces that the number of MIUI users has reached 50 million.
- June 10: The activity "Like Xiaomi Service Month" begins with service being provided by 18 Mi Homes and more than 500 authorized service stations around the country, all providing rapid-repair service within an hour, free phone/films service, free maintenance service outside insurance, and other forms of preferential, high-quality service.

ILLUSTRATIONS

Chapter 3

Chapter 4

Chapter 5

Chapter 6

Chapter 7

ACKNOWLEDGMENTS

THE BENEFACTORS OF
THIS PARTICULAR DREAM

Thank you to all of the following friends who made this book possible:

Left from top to bottom: Jin Cuodao, advisor; Liang Feng, designer; Chen Lu, designer; and Long Tao, illustrator
Middle from top to bottom: Xu Jieyun, marketing; Yao Liang, planning; Yan Chao, illustrator; and Ni Yan, illustrator
Right from top to bottom: Zhao Gang, marketing; Diao Meiling, product; Wang Yanchao, illustrator; and Alee's friends, proofreaders

Transmitter groups, 94
Transparency, 101–102
Tribes of fans, 66
Trust, 11–12, 140–142

UGC (user-generated content), 16
Ultimate excellence:
  achieving, 41–45
  in four-word formula for Internet
    businesses, 5
  in product mentality, 55
  and word-of-mouth reputation, 9
Upgrades:
  activities related to, 41
  to internal office systems, 161–163
Usefulness, in content operations, 107
User events, 67–72
User experience:
  and content operations, 107
  and craftsmanship, 42–44
  at Kingsoft, 2
  understanding users to design, 31–37
User groups, on Weibo vs. BBSs, 130,
  131
User interface/user experience (UI/UE)
  (see User experience)
User relations, 111
User-generated content (UGC), 16
Users:
  customer service focused on,
    139–144
  development with, 48–49
  gifts from, 51–52
  identifying/understanding, 31–37,
    198
  influence on product development
    team of, 48–52
  making friends with, 12–14, 140
  models by engineering staff vs.,
    23–26
  opening R&D to, 19, 26
  product assembly by, 86–87
  ranking demands of, 29–31
  relationships between, 132
  in three-on-three principles of
    engagement, 18

Valentine's Day, advertising related to,
  179, 180
Value-added business, 106
Values, of consumers, 216
VANCL, 57
Videos, 192, 204

Wang Wei, 75
Wang Yangming, 231
"Watch ad, Like, Smash golden egg,
  Win awards" activity, 93
"Water-buffalo" systems, 39
The Water-Lily Pond (Monet), 220
We Media:
  content for, 107–109
  product managers on, 110–111
  in three-on-three principles of
    engagement, 18, 105
  traditional media and, 95, 106–107
  WeChat in, 126
Wearable devices, 211
Website(s):
  bullet curtain, 203–204
  channeling traffic on, 40
  features on, 80–82
  images on, 190–192
WeChat, 7, 8, 125–129
  Bomb Plane game on, 115
  customer service via, 148, 156
  marketing on, 97
  other social media channels vs.,
    110–112
  "Our Age" ad on, 93
  in We Media matrix, 108, 109
  word-of-mouth promotion on, 19
  Xiaomi users on, 112
WeChat Lucky Money (activity), 19
Weibo, 7, 13, 112–122
  accommodating characteristics of,
    128
  activity on, 105
  BBSs vs., 129–130
  customer service via, 147, 148, 156
  discussions of Mi TV on, 176
  "Fried chicken and beer" promotion
    on, 121–122